CH
SUPER
PSYCHICS

CHINA'S SUPER PSYCHICS

Paul Dong and Thomas E. Raffill

Marlowe & Company
New York

Published by
Marlowe & Company
632 Broadway, Seventh Floor
New York NY 10012

Library of Congress Cataloging in Publication Data 97-74218

ISBN 1-56924-715-3

Manufactured in the United States of America
First Edition

Contents

CONTENTS

• Foreword •

by Karen S. Kramer, Ph.D.

Psychic phenomena have been part of my life since child-hood. My introduction to chi gong came in 1988, in relation to a health issue. The relationship between the two, chi gong and the psychic, came during my first trip to China in 1992. The story begins in 1987 when I had emergency surgery fol-lowing a colonoscopy in which the snare used to remove polyps became entangled in the fibrous polyp located in my colon. The only option was to have the instrument surgically removed. This was fortunate as the polyp proved to be can-cerous. So, along with the removal of the scope and snare, nine inches of my colon and all diseased tissue were removed. It is important to report that today I am cancer-free and have been since the surgery. Chi gong gets the credit for my cur-rent and lasting state of extreme good health.

Now to my introduction to chi gong. In preparing for my first follow-up colonoscopy, I was concerned that I not be required to take the tranquilizing medication often adminis-tered for this procedure. I was also aware that my ascending colon was quite twisted with adhesions resulting from my rigorous play shortly after a childhood appendectomy. For this reason, the doctor was insisting that I be prepared to take the medication. After consultation with a hypnotherapist friend about the condition, I followed his advice and contacted an acupressurist. I explained the problem and was met with the reply, "I will straighten your colon." Well, what had I to lose? I made an appointment and enjoyed a wonderfully gentle acupressure massage four days before the scheduled colonoscopy. I felt little but did notice that the man waved his hands over my abdomen a few times.

The day of the colonoscopy came and I presented myself for the procedure. After insisting that my colon was terribly twisted, the doctor finally relented and allowed me to proceed using only my hypnosis tape. The doctor then came to face me, arms akimbo, and reported in a hostile tone, "I don't know what you've done, but your colon is no longer twisted!" When I replied, "I'll tell you," I was cut off by his rapid backward retreat from the room, hands waving in front of his face, saying, "I don't want to know." Perhaps he felt that I had engaged in some sort of black magic.

Needless to say, I was an instant "true believer" in the power of external chi treatment and chi gong. I continued to visit the acupressurist as a client and ultimately became a pupil of chi gong. In 1992, an opportunity to study chi gong in China arose. This is when I experienced the connection between chi gong and psychic phenomena and this trip also introduced me to Paul Dong. In preparation for the trip to China in 1992, we were provided with a reading list. Paul's book, *Chi Gong—The Ancient Chinese Way to Health*, published in 1990 by Marlowe and Company, was one of the recommended texts.

The context for my psychic experience begins just prior to departing for China. One of my pet cats became seriously ill. His behavior became strange and fearful, his eyes were all pupil. The vet seemed to help initially, but the problems returned as I was leaving for China. I left him in the care of good friends. The cat had to be returned to the vet and I had to call the vet to determine what could be done. When I talked with the vet, he reported that the animal was responding slightly to medication and that he would be watched for twenty-four hours. If there was no significant improvement, or a decline, the vet recommended that the animal be put to sleep. With heavy heart, I gave my permission for the vet to proceed as he felt appropriate.

The morning after my phone conversation, our group rose early for a daylong excursion. We were on the road before five A.M. As we rode along in the dark, I began to meditate on my cat, sending him healing energy. The woman I was sitting with joined me in this effort. Then I saw my cat lying on the metal exam table, *and I saw him go limp.* I was quite upset but continued to send loving energy. Immediately I saw him sit up, shake himself, and begin grooming. My companion also felt a surge of positive energy in her meditation. I hoped against hope that he had received the energy and was on the road to recovery. Of course, a couple of days later, I got a phone call reporting that the cat had been put to sleep. It was then that I began to realize what I had seen. I had actually been present with my sweet loving animal when he received the lethal injection, and I had also witnessed his spirit break free from the confines of the diseased and now dead body. I truly felt that he had become a free and happy animal again.

When I returned home, I was able to meet with the vet. We discussed my visions and I reported what time it had been in China and calculated what time it had been in California. The vet was amazed. My experience had occurred exactly at the time he had injected my cat. I am certain that working with the chi in our daily practices and being in the chi-rich environment of China, along with my caring for my pet, opened my psychic senses to allow me to be with him at that time.

After returning home, I was able to find a copy of Paul's book and avidly read it. I was deeply inspired and longed to meet this unique individual. Although he lives and works in a nearby community, the opportunity to meet did not occur until early in 1996. I had been asked to work with a chi gong master from Hangzhou, the city I have visited five times now to study chi gong. When I arrived at the San Francisco office of this chi gong master early one morning, another man was present. To my honor and delight, I was introduced to Paul Dong, the man I had admired since reading his book in 1992. Since that time we have exchanged information on psychic experiences independent of and in connection with chi gong. I am delighted to be able to write the foreword to Paul's latest book on psychic phenomena and chi.

In my several trips to China and in my practice of chi gong here in California, I have found that the connection to universal energy is enhanced by the practice of chi gong. It indeed affords one an opportunity to have many unusual experiences which can only be described as psychic. The Chinese scientists have studied these connections for decades. I encourage you to explore this report of the scientific study of such phenomena, which has taken place in China over time and which continues today.

I thank Paul Dong for the opportunity to share one of my personal experiences with you. Paul is a wonderful scholar and a longtime practitioner of chi gong. It is inspirational to know him.

• 1 •

China's Super Psychics

The date is January 3, 1987; the place, Beijing. Inside the Chinese Communist Party Central Committee Training Center for Province-Level Cadres, a strange spectacle is unfolding before the eyes of the approximately thirty witnesses in the room.

"Bring in the bottle!"

In answer to the command, someone brings in a bottle filled with medicine pills of various kinds.

The official clerk inspects the bottle and certifies that it has never been opened, the cork is firmly in place, the wax seal is intact, and the plastic bottlecap is sitting securely on top.

"All right, you may proceed!"

The bottle is handed over to a man, who quietly concentrates his entire being on it.

Soon afterward, forty-four medicine pills are transported out of the bottle. The experiment in "psychokinesis" (moving

Author, Paul Dong

objects with the mind) is a success. The main character in this scene is Zhang Baosheng, a man around thirty years old who is one of mainland China's super psychics. Famous for his prankish personality, Baosheng not only moved the pills out of the bottle as he was supposed to, this time he also sent into the bottle one piece of candy.

The Chinese government places great importance on people like Zhang Baosheng. Such people, gifted with what the Chinese have termed "exceptional human functions" (abbreviated as EHF from here on), are viewed as national treasures. Baosheng himself often demonstrates his amazing powers for visiting foreign dignitaries and on Chinese television, and he is a nationwide celebrity in China.

As a national treasure, Baosheng not only commands the respect of his countrymen, he also receives a number of privileges, including the status of being under national protection. This means, among other things, that for his transportation he has Chinese secret service bodyguards who drive him in police cars of the latest models—a rare privilege indeed in mainland China.

With his medium height, Baosheng looks ordinary, but everyone who meets him is in awe of him and his fantastic abilities. They'd better be, because Baosheng's greatest pleasure is to play practical jokes on people who don't respect him enough. He has been known to pat a person on the shoulder and use his power to let his handprint sink into the person's skin, leaving a mark which cannot be washed off.

Once, when Baosheng wanted to go out, there were no new cars available, so Baosheng was stuck with an old, run-down car.

"What happened to my car?" Baosheng disappointedly asked one of his bodyguards, who was serving as his chauffeur.

"I—I'm sorry, Mr. Zhang, sir," the bodyguard explained, "but high-ranking officials in the security bureau have taken all the new ones. There—there's nothing I can do."

"Is that so? Well, watch out. If this happens again, there'll *really* be nothing you can do!" Baosheng's tone was becoming more threatening. "And you'd better not make any trouble about this, because if I hear about it, I'll move a coin into your stomach!"

With these words he asked the other bodyguard, sitting next to him, to feel the change in his pocket. He was unnerved to discover that the coins had disappeared from his pocket without a trace, and they turned up in the pocket of the chauffeur. The two bodyguards were scared out of their wits and didn't dare say a word.

However, Baosheng's psychic ability is more than just an amusing plaything. The Chinese government is very serious about its top-secret scientific and military research program on psychic abilities. Besides the test at the Central Committee Training Center described earlier, there is at least one other documented instance of a psychokinesis demonstration by Baosheng. For China's Ministry of Space Industries (this space exploration agency is China's equivalent to NASA), Baosheng used psychokinesis to move pills out through the mouth of a tightly sealed medicine bottle. The scientists filmed this demonstration using high-speed photography (400 frames per second). One pill showed up halfway through the mouth of the bottle.

A personal acquaintance of mine, Mrs. Chyung Yao, had a memorable encounter with Zhang Baosheng (Here, and throughout the book, the speaker is Paul Dong). Chyung Yao, a famous writer living in Taiwan, often communicates with me by mail. I have the highest regard for her literary achievements (she has written over twenty-five novels, over half of which have been made into movies and videos), as well as her great personal integrity. Chyung Yao is so popular, mainland China has announced that several publishing houses will jointly publish her novels, with an estimated ten million copies to be printed. Her husband, Ping Syin-Tau, is the publisher and manager of *Crown*, a widely respected monthly magazine in Taiwan. These two most reliable and qualified witnesses have reported the following little incident about Zhang Baosheng.

As a novelist, Chyung Yao always felt a deep longing to return to her homeland, to see the scenes of the villages, the countryside, and the nature which form her roots. However, for over thirty years this had been impossible because of the abysmal state of relations between mainland China and Taiwan (both the Communist regime on the mainland and the Nationalist regime on Taiwan claim to be the legitimate government of all China). But more recently, there has been a thaw of sorts in relations between the rival governments of China. Mainland China launched a new "charm offensive" aimed at projecting a more friendly image toward Taiwan, and in 1987 Taiwan removed its ban on travel to mainland China by private citizens. As a result, Chyung Yao's dream of returning to the mainland for a visit came true in early spring of 1988.

As Chyung Yao described it in her article "My Trip to Mainland China" (*Crown* 414): After she landed in mainland China, she was greeted by some of her relatives. Of course, they had much to talk about during this emotional reunion, but eventually the conversation turned to the question of what to see.

Chyung Yao has a relative named Miss Chu Xia, who suggested that she see the amazing Zhang Baosheng. She said he had special powers, could move objects with his mind, could make an apple several miles away fly into his hand, and could do many other things difficult to describe. She shouldn't miss out on this!

Chyung Yao indicated that she had come here to see the sights of her native country, not to meet some legendary wonderman. But in the end, she gave in to the appeals of her relatives and agreed to go see Zhang Baosheng.

Actually, Chyung Yao's relatives had always wanted to see Zhang Baosheng in person, but not just anybody could get the chance to do that. Now, with Chyung Yao's special status as an honored visitor, they figured their chance had come. As a matter of fact, the authorities in mainland China were eager to give the influential writer Chyung Yao everything she wanted, in accordance with the "smiling-face policy," their latest tactic for dealing with Taiwan. So, when Chyung Yao expressed a wish to see Zhang Baosheng, the authorities agreed.

Chyung Yao and her relatives waited a long time for Zhang Baosheng's appearance, but he kept them waiting. They were becoming a little anxious. While they were waiting, she heard many more stories about Zhang Baosheng.

Then, the coordinator for this meeting told Chyung Yao and her family that Zhang Baosheng was making a fuss. He wanted to come through Tiananmen, but only visiting foreign dignitaries are allowed to come that way. They were arguing with him, but he absolutely refused to come unless he could come through Tiananmen.

Chyung Yao was astonished by this. Tiananmen (Gate of Heavenly Peace) is the symbol of authority to the Chinese. Built by the Mongol emperor Kublai Khan in 1271, this gigantic entrance to the Imperial Palace has always been used by the dictators of China as a place to show their absolute power over the people. Under the Communists, high-ranking government and party officials have used it as a reviewing stand for their endless military parades celebrating their mighty regime. That is why Chyung Yao couldn't believe Zhang Baosheng was asking to come through this gate.

Chyung Yao was fascinated by this situation. By now, she was also eager to meet this amazing person. Finally Zhang Baosheng arrived, along with his wife. They all went into the room assigned for the meeting, expressed their admiration to Baosheng, and respectfully indicated that they wished he would show them some of his abilities. Baosheng hesitated briefly, and then he pointed to a young lady among them and commanded her to take off her clothes!

Chyung Yao said the young lady was stunned. She didn't dare oppose Zhang Baosheng, but she couldn't undress in front of everybody, either. In Chinese culture, women are more conservative and more protective of their purity than in the liberated West. The young lady just stood there wondering what to do. Fortunately, Chyung Yao's husband convinced Baosheng to do the demonstration with some other lady's garments. Baosheng shot an annoyed glance at the lady, but then he touched the garment they had provided and kneaded it in his hands. The garment started giving off smoke, then burst into flames.

Out of her thirty-three-page report, "My Trip to Mainland China," Chyung Yao spent ten pages reporting on the amazing abilities of Zhang Baosheng. Of course, this included a description of his EHF power of removing medicine pills from a sealed bottle. This ability is not unique to Zhang Baosheng. Many psychics in China can remove medicine pills from sealed bottles. What I find more interesting is that after Baosheng emptied all the pills from the bottle with his mind, he moved into the bottle a crumpled-up slip of paper on which Chyung Yao had written the Chinese character *shuang* ("pair"). She brought it back with her to Taiwan, and now, in her idle moments, she often turns the bottle over and studies it. She still cannot understand how those pills got out and how the slip of paper got in.

Zhang Baosheng's strange EHF often leaves people wondering afterward. Chyung Yao is not alone in this. The well-known Chinese scholar Qian Jiaju has a similar tale to tell those of us interested in EHF. He revealed to friends that he wrote a few words on a blank piece of paper with nobody watching, and sealed it in an envelope. Zhang Baosheng not only knew what he had written, he also sent a piece of candy into the envelope. "I have kept the inexplicable envelope to this day as a souvenir," said Qian.

Zhang Baosheng's EHF is first-class. However, China has people with even more amazing powers, considered "top secret class." There are few such "top secret class" people gifted with EHF. These people are not well known, they never appear in public, and they are under the "special protection" of the government. They serve as the subjects of secret scientific and military research. It is rumored that one of them can move huge objects, and another can cause a normal person's blood pressure to rise to a dangerous level, or cause the eyes, ears, nose, and mouth to spurt blood, from hundreds of miles away.

On this brief visit to mainland China, Chyung Yao only had time to scratch the surface. What she saw was only a tiny part of Zhang Baosheng's strange abilities. Everyone hopes to get a chance to meet a celebrity like Zhang Baosheng, including myself. In this regard, I greatly appreciate the assistance of the father of Yao Zheng, a lady with EHF (*see chapter 11*). In November 1990 he helped me arrange to see Zhang Baosheng in the guest room of his residence. When I arrived, he was out entertaining guests. I had to wait all of forty-five minutes for him to return with his two bodyguards in military uniform, who were carrying pistols and cordless phones.

Also present were his leader, Mr. Zhai (a political commissar for an army division), and several military men. They were chatting with each other and took no notice of me. I repeatedly asked Mr. Zhai to let me see a demonstration of Zhang Baosheng's powers. I wouldn't have minded even if he used his powers to burn my three-hundred-dollar suit. That would have been a nice souvenir for me.

Mr. Zhai asked Zhang Baosheng for me, but Zhang ignored him. All Mr. Zhai could do was apologize for him, saying he may have been tired after going out with his guests. When he is tired, his powers do not work. This seemed quite reasonable to me. Usually, Zhang meets famous people. Since I wasn't famous, it would stand to reason that he wouldn't do a demonstration for me. I also knew about his bad temper and his tendency to make scenes. If he doesn't like you, he won't let you photograph him. If you try to take pictures anyway, he can use his powers to make your camera malfunction or break. This is why, in writing this book, I don't have even one photo of him.

Zhang refused to do a demonstration for me, but I was not disappointed. I am not the first to have been refused by him. Zhang is famous for his bad temper and capriciousness. It is said that he once had a tantrum that went all the way to China's top leader. Sources report that one day in Zhongnanhai (a place in Beijing where all the top leaders live), a group of high-ranking officials were waiting for Zhang Baosheng to give an EHF demonstration. Perhaps he wasn't in the right mood for it, or was having a fit of temper. The officials waited thirty minutes for him, but couldn't see his demonstration. This was too disrespectful.

Then, the highest leader among them ordered that he be locked up in a room. When this official went home, as soon as he opened his door, he saw Zhang Baosheng waiting there for him. He was stunned. From that time on, Zhang Baosheng has been working for China's Defense Ministry. To those who think it is impossible to walk through walls, I would ask the following question. If pills can go through bottles, why can't a person's body go through a wall? Because Zhang has such high-level abilities, one foreign government sent an agent to China to offer Zhang twenty million dollars to invite him to their country for "research" activities. He refused.

Since the 1980s, Professor Song Kongzhi has been doing research in human body sciences, including many experiments on people with EHF. He has revealed that Zhang has the power to move shoes, hot-water bottles, keys, and other objects through wooden boards and walls and make large objects move back and forth. On one occasion, before a large number of witnesses, Zhang caused a hundred-pound sack of sugar to move through the walls of a storehouse, ending up in front of them. This was seen by EHF researcher Mr. He Ren of Heilongjiang University and Dr. He Yannian of Beijing's Institute for Research in Chinese Medicine. One source for this story is Assistant Professor Lin Weihuang of the physics department of Beijing Teachers' College. He is said to have discussed it in a newly organized colloquium on human body science in the spring 1988 semester, arousing great interest among the students in attendance.

Besides his bad temper and tendency for making scenes, Zhang Baosheng also loves to play practical jokes. But sometimes he takes things too far and plays the sort of joke that could curdle your stomach or make your hair stand on end. Tao Le, a former columnist for Hong Kong's newspaper, *Ming Pao*, and a member of Hong Kong's Institute for Research in

Ancient Oriental Anomalies, has made many trips, both on his own and as an organizer of a group, to Beijing to investigate and interview people with EHF. One time, he brought a group to Beijing to visit Zhang Baosheng. After their meal, Zhang Baosheng played a big joke. A three-carat diamond ring worn by a lady in the group, a movie starlet from Hong Kong, flew away by itself. She was in great distress and didn't know what to do. She thought it must have been Zhang Baosheng playing tricks, so she asked Tao Le to plead with him. With a laugh, Zhang Baosheng pointed to a spot beneath a nearby flowerpot and said that's where the diamond ring went. The diamond ring, with a sale value of tens of thousands of U.S. dollars, was returned to its original owner, who thanked her lucky stars for it.

Zhang Baosheng is also called "the little god." After he received a gift of a luxury auto from Hong Kong billionaire Li Jiacheng (the richest man in Hong Kong), he took to driving it around town, but he often broke the traffic rules and got tickets. Baosheng takes his tickets with a smile, but when the traffic officers return to the station, they can never find the tickets, which have disappeared without a trace. Since he became known for this, police officers get out of the way when they see his car coming. Nobody dares to bother him anymore. He is a "national treasure," and he can make traffic tickets disappear too. Who would want to pick a fight with him?

Zhang Baosheng grew up poor and never had enough to eat. Even though he has been elevated to the status of "national treasure," battalion commander in the army, owner of a luxury car, and the subject of a ten-million-dollar research effort, he hasn't forgotten the impoverished conditions of his childhood.

When he is invited to dinner, he remembers the ancient

wisdom—"A piece of cloth, a bowl of rice, people should know how hard these are to come by." For this reason, he doesn't let people order too many dishes in his presence. If the dishes have already been ordered, he insists that none of the food is wasted. Nobody dares to go against this "order" of his. Otherwise, he will give a puff, and send the food he wants you to eat right into your stomach, like it or not. Chyung Yao, the lady writer mentioned earlier, suffered this experience.

All who have met Zhang Baosheng know that one of his remarkable powers is "restoring a card." On one occasion, several people offered him their business card. He picked one out and said, "All right, put your card in your mouth. That's right, now chew it up. You've got it? Now spit it out." Baosheng took the spit-out bits of the card and mashed them into a ball. After a while, he said, "Uh-oh, I don't have the whole card here. There are some more bits inside of you!"

The person stirred his tongue around in his mouth and managed to retrieve a few more bits of the card, and within moments the card was restored to its original condition. The group of spectators around him burst into applause.

Today, Zhang Baosheng is a battalion commander (in rank and privilege, but without an actual battalion). However, it is not generally known that he has also worked as a public safety officer. About eight years ago, his rich psychic powers had not yet manifested themselves. At that time, he only had a few lesser abilities such as reading with the ear and seeing through clothes. When the local authorities discovered these powers, they gave him a low-level security job. All he did was ride the bus and catch thieves. Because his ears and eyes are extremely sensitive, he can sense or observe the movements of the thieves, and he often made use of his EHF abilities to catch them on the bus.

One day, Zhang Baosheng was on duty on a bus. Suddenly, an image opened in his mind, like a TV screen. The image was of a hand going into a man's pocket, and slowly taking out a wad of cash. Immediately, Zhang started squeezing his way through the crowd (the busses in mainland China are packed), and grabbed the thief. At this point, I'd like to add that many people in mainland China with EHF have reported that when they read with the hands or with the ear, guess things, or see through objects, the mind forms something like a screen with an image of the target being sought. Sometimes the target flashes by in an instant, sometimes it is quite fuzzy, and sometimes it is sharp and clear.

When he started working on the buses, Zhang Baosheng caught many thieves. He was beginning to build a reputation and a name for himself. His fame spread, and people in the underworld wanted to "teach him a lesson." Then tragedy came on the heels of success. He met a girlfriend on the bus, a lady named Xiao Yuan, a lab technician in a factory. They began dating each other seriously.

One day, Zhang Baosheng saw a young lady walking in the street. The lady had on high-heeled shoes. They matched her attractive figure and were a fine sight. Zhang Baosheng's thoughts turned to his girlfriend.

"Xiao Yuan would look nicer in high heels," he thought, but he couldn't afford even a small item like that on his salary. In any case, he felt like going to a shoe shop to take a look. To satisfy himself, he went to a shop called Xihu Shoe Store. Its shelves were stocked with all kinds of shoes, but there was a pair of lady's shoes that he particularly liked. He thought and thought about it. . . .

Because he thought about that pair of shoes fixedly, as he was leaving the shop, he noticed that his bag had got heavier. He looked inside, and to his great surprise, the lady's shoes were in it. In that instant of confusion, he had no chance to think. He stepped out the door, but just then he heard a voice from behind—the shop attendant shouting, "Grab him!" He was immediately surrounded by a crowd of shop clerks and shoppers. He was so ashamed he wanted to hide, and he didn't know how to explain himself. Everyone thought he was a thief. The police were summoned, and they brought him to the station.

Zhang Baosheng always caught thieves, but he never imagined that he would one day be taken for a thief and caught himself.

When he was in prison and there was nothing he could do, he felt terribly humiliated. But the material evidence at the time was irrefutable. Besides, he was also terrified and confused by his powers. Why would those lady's shoes run into his bag? He couldn't imagine the answer at that moment.

It was only after he finished serving his sentence and was released from jail that an EHF researcher told him that he may have strengthened his EHF through repeated use of it on his job as a watchman on the bus, and in that way he may have developed the power of "psychokinesis." After that, if he thought, *"Apple,"* an apple would come to his hand. Whatever he would think about, that's what he would get.

A friend of mine in Hong Kong, Mr. Zhang Qunmo, is a columnist and science-fiction writer. In his science-fiction novel *Yi Ren* (*Unusual Person*), published in Hong Kong in 1990, he has a character called Jin Xiaobao, in many ways based on Zhang Baosheng. The book is filled with EHF episodes taken from actual things that are known about Zhang Baosheng. In one scene, an old man is selling persimmons. When Jin Xiaobao walks by and shouts, "Shoo, shoo!" the persimmons in the old man's basket inexplicably start disappearing one by one. "He tried to grab hold of them right away, but it was no use." The basket was emptied of its persimmons.

That is how powerful Zhang Baosheng's EHF is. There is certainly enough material about him to fill a whole book.

• 2 •

Professor Qian Xuesen Supports
Psychic Research

Since March 1979, when the Chinese first recognized the existence of EHF, researchers from around the country responded by taking up this problem. This included a large number of scientists, and among these was Qian Xuesen, known as China's "father of the missile." Qian Xuesen is one of China's top scientists and holds many important national responsibilities. How could he have the leisure time to become interested in this? Let us see how Qian Xuesen answered a question posed by a reporter for the Hong Kong newspaper *Wen Hui Bao*.

"I hear you believe in EHF, so I have come to ask you about it," said the reporter.

"At first I didn't believe in it. I came to believe in it after seeing it with my own eyes," he said. Then he explained to the reporter that he saw an EHF demonstration with a sealed bottle of medicine pills held in the hand. There were a hundred pills inside. Then, thirty-three pills fell into the hand. When he opened the bottle and counted, there were seventy-seven pills left inside. It was simply a fact, and he was convinced. He also mentioned an EHF demonstration his team gave for a government leader. The leader made a very scientific comment: There are things not yet understood, but not things beyond all possible understanding. (Actually that is a quote from Lenin.) This means we need to do research on those things we do not yet understand.

Qian Xuesen also said that those who persist in the research will definitely make some discovery. When they do, the researchers will know that they have gone far beyond the boundaries of the current scientific knowledge.

Qian Xuesen is a scientist. He is definitely not the sort of person who would believe in something like EHF after seeing only one or two demonstrations. He is firmly convinced of the reality of EHF because he has personally observed many demonstrations, tests, and experiments. The test he mentioned above is only one example. Another striking example occurred one time when Qian Xuesen was with quantum physicists Professor Tang Jiaoyan and Professor Zhang Weijiao. Zhang Baosheng pointed at Zhang Weijiao with his hand, and a hole was burned in his shirt. Afterward, Professor Tang said he might be able to explain this burning phenomenon as some sort of effect of electromagnetic waves. For example, the electromagnetic waves emitted by Zhang Baosheng could excite the molecules in the shirt, leading to an air friction effect, creating heat and burning a hole in it. When Qian Xuesen saw this with his own eyes, how could he have any doubts?

Qian Xuesen not only believes in EHF, he also thinks EHF phenomena can be explained with our present-day physics. For example, psychokinesis could be an effect of electromagnetic fields and waves. He tells a very interesting story in this regard. In World War II, it was discovered that some workers in radar stations had the ability to "hear" microwave signals. It seemed uncanny, but later, the reason became clear. It turned out that electromagnetic waves were being absorbed in the head unevenly. This gave rise to sound waves that could be heard. This example explains away the "exceptional" aspect of exceptional human functions, and shows that it is possible to find out the reasons for EHF through research.

When discussing human body energy, we must also turn to the subject of chi gong (energy meditation), which is currently very popular in China. I am a chi gong practitioner myself and have already published two books on the subject in England and the U.S. As explained in one of these, called *Chi Gong—The Ancient Chinese Way to Health* (Marlowe and Company, 1990), chi gong is primarily for health promotion. However, long practice of chi gong can also give rise to psychic phenomena. Yan Xin, discussed in chapter 6, is an example of a person who developed world-class psychic abilities from chi gong.

When a person has reached a high stage of chi gong practice, the internal body produces a strong chi energy flow. This energy can be released through the eyes, palms, or fingers. In the terminology of chi gong, this is called energy healing. While the power can be used for healing, it can also be used to harm the body. This is the "empty force" used in chi gong for martial arts. The helpful or harmful direction of the power is determined by the mind and the strength of the "chi" energy developed through practice.

We know that the "chi" of chi gong is closely related to the chi or energy of EHF. Since Zhang Baosheng is a top EHF man, his mind and chi energy are far stronger than most people's. Thus, when he thinks of burning your clothes, his chi (or electromagnetic waves) will generate friction with the air molecules, the smoke will rise, and then burst into flames.

When Qian Xuesen was talking with the reporter in the interview mentioned above, he also discussed this link between chi gong and EHF. "We have discovered that people with EHF are in certain respects similar to chi gong practitioners. When someone with EHF gives a demonstration, in the same manner as when a chi gong practitioner releases energy, the face turns red and the forehead sweats." As Qian Xuesen explains, "We did experiments taking electroencephalograms, and we discovered that the brain patterns of chi gong masters giving out energy are very similar to those of people with EHF during tests of their abilities. This shows a connection between chi gong and EHF."

Qian Xuesen also believes that, since chi gong is based on the same theory as Chinese medicine, chi gong, Chinese medicine and EHF must be the same thing, and EHF is just one of the more striking manifestations of that "thing." He has indicated that to develop EHF, chi gong, and Chinese medicine into true scientific theories, we need to make a breakthrough going beyond the current science.

He has made the far-reaching statement, "The ultimate result of work in Chinese medicine, chi gong, and EHF will be a new scientific revolution. When that happens, it could be called the Oriental scientific revolution!" Similarly, in the Third Plenary Session of the Planning Committee for the Chinese Human Body Research Conference he gave a report on the theme, "Can This Give Birth to a New Scientific Revolution?" In his conclusion, he said, "Human body science may lead to a new scientific revolution in the twenty-first century, one that may be bigger than the revolutions brought by quantum mechanics and relativity in the early twentieth century.

Fig. 2–1
Professor Qian Xuesen (fourth from left in the front row) talked to the media in Beijing, July 1980, on the importance of studying EHF. This photo was taken after the conference. (photo courtesy of Zhou Wen Bin)

Who among us will be the originators of this future revolution?"

From reading the above reports, we can all see what an important role Qian Xuesen plays in the progress of EHF research in China. Thus, for a deeper understanding of China's EHF research, we must first understand who Qian Xuesen is. To say no more than the one sentence, "Qian Xuesen is one of China's top scientists," as in the preceding section, is not enough. We must look at his full background if we wish to understand the general direction and focus of China's EHF research.

Qian Xuesen (while studying in the U.S. his name was spelled as Tsien, Hsue Shen) was born in 1911 in Shanghai. In 1934, he graduated from the department of railroad mechanical engineering at Shanghai's Jiaotong University. In 1935, he went to the U.S. to study aeronautical engineering at the Massachusetts Institute of Technology (MIT), receiving a master's degree. In 1936, he moved to the California Institute of Technology to pursue further studies, attaining a doctorate in aerodynamics in 1939.

His mentor was a founder of modern dynamics, Professor Theodore Von Karman. Dr. Qian was an important member of the earliest rocketry research institute organized by Karman, the Guggenheim Jet Propulsion Laboratory in the California Institute of Technology, and he served as director of this research center as well. The supersonic flow concept first proposed by him and Karman was basic to aerodynamics, and the well-known Karman-Qian formula was used for the aerodynamics of high subsonic aircraft, a major contribution.

In addition, during the 1940s, in collaboration with Dr. F. Malina, Dr. Qian established theoretical foundations for surface-to-surface missiles and surveillance rockets, as well as doing pioneering work for the U.S. in the use of composite-propellant rocket engines. In these regards, Dr. Qian created a valuable basis for further developments in aerodynamics and rocketry in the U.S.

During World War II, he was the head of the missile unit of the science advisory committee for the U.S. National Defense. As an official representative of the U.S. government, he led a team of experts to postwar Germany to assess the role of German scientists in missile development during the war. Because of Qian Xuesen's ability, the U.S. government considered using him for nuclear research, but this was during the period of McCarthyite hysteria, and Qian Xuesen had been involved with the Communist Party in an earlier period, so his appointment was dropped and instead he was tasked with the theoretical study of sending a man to the moon.

When Qian Xuesen applied for U.S. citizenship, the authorities refused it, but had no proof that he was a Communist agent. This damaged Qian's reputation and career. Thus, in the autumn of 1949, Dr. Qian and his wife, Jiang Ying, made the decision to return to their native country, China. However, the U.S. authorities strongly opposed this as well. Dr. Qian could never have imagined that his enormous achievements and contributions would become an obstacle to his returning home to China. In the spring of 1950, when Dr. Qian and his wife tried to board a flight in Los Angeles leaving for Canada, he was detained by immigration authorities. His ten-plus bags of books and notes were confiscated.

Five years later, Communist China's Premier Zhou Enlai applied his skills in negotiations with the U.S., and received Dr. Qian in exchange for eleven U.S. pilots captured in the Korean War. At the time, a rear admiral in the U.S. Department of Defense said, "The exchange is like five American divisions for eleven pilots." (It could be inferred that Qian Xuesen was an asset worth five divisions to a country's defense.)

After Dr. Qian returned to his homeland, Chairman Mao Zedong met him and asked him to train scientists for China, Premier Zhou Enlai asked for his opinions on how to develop science and technology, and the first thing General Chen Geng said to him was, "Can China build its own missiles?" Dr. Qian said, "The Chinese people are not stupid. Of course they can." Thus, he presented to the Chinese government a *Proposal for the Development of a Defense Aerospace Industry.* From then on, he became involved in the long-term guidance of China's rocketry, missile, and space technology research and development.

In October 1966, the eleventh year after Dr. Qian's return, China successfully tested an atomic warhead launched on a guided missile to a distance of 644 kilometers. In April 1970, China sent up its first satellite. In May 1980, China shot an intercontinental ballistic missile a distance of 10,000 kilometers, instantly shaking the world. An editorial in a U.S. newspaper implied that China's ICBM firing was Qian Xuesen's victory. Then, in 1981, China for the first time launched three satellites simultaneously. In October 1982, China successfully fired a guided missile from a submarine in waters north of Taiwan. Since that time, China has been the third-strongest missile power after the U.S. and Russia.

Today, Dr. Qian is chairman of the Chinese Scientists' Association, executive chairman of the Chinese Academy of Sciences, and president of the Society of System Engineering of China and the Chinese Society of Astronautics. He is also the honorary president of the Chinese Human Body Science Research Society. He has been the leader of almost all fields of science in China. In China, people may not know who the current leaders are, but all know who Qian Xuesen is.

And what of his international standing? In August 1989, Qian Xuesen won the Willard F. Rockwell, Jr. medal, the highest award given by the International Technology Institute of the United States. Others who shared the honor of winning this award were "the father of the Hydrogen Bomb," Dr. Edward Teller of the U.S., and French physicist Robert Klapisch. Recipients of the award must be people of extremely high stature in the international scientific community and electable to the world level of the Hall of Fame for engineering, science, and technology. Dr. Qian's awards give recognition to his enormous pioneering contributions to rocketry, guided missiles, aerospace technology, and systems science in China.

As honorary president of the Chinese Human Body Science Research Society, Dr. Qian gives direct leadership to EHF or psychic research. By understanding his background and his level of knowledge, we can appraise the prospects of China's EHF research, and come to appreciate its breadth and depth.

Paul Dong and Thomas Raffill

Having reviewed Dr. Qian's career, we are in a position to look at his pronouncements and publications, as well as his actions in support of China's EHF research.

Since the beginning of the EHF boom in China in 1979, Qian Xuesen has authored many research papers and lectures. A brief bibliography of these follows, to give us some idea of his thinking and viewpoints.

Reports on EHF

"EHF Research Has Great Meaning." *Beijing Keji (Beijing Science and Technology)*, July 18, 1980.

"This is the Birth of a New Scientific Revolution." *EHF Yanjiu (EHF Research)*, vol. 1, 1983. [Note: This research organization's journal is for internal distribution only. It is not for sale, and its export to foreign countries is prohibited.]

"EHF and Society." *EHF Yanjiu*, vol. 3, 1983.

"Our Research Work Should Give Equal Weight to Experiment and Theory." *EHF Yanjiu*, vols. 1 and 2, 1985.

"EHF and New Scientific Fields." *Renmin Zhengxie Bao (Reports of the People's Political Consultative Conference)*, May 23, 1986.

"On EHF Research." Speech at the organizing meeting for the Human Body Science Specialists Association, October 9, 1987.

Reports on Traditional Chinese Medicine and Chi Gong Theory

"Three Letters on Research to Modernize Chinese Medicine." August 3, 1980. [Three letters from Qian Xuesen to EHF researchers.]

Fig. 2–2
A bimonthly magazine of *Exceptional Human Function Research* is for members only, not for sale, and not allowed to be sent out of the country. It is a sister publication of the *Chinese Journal of Somatic Science.*

"Chi Gong Can Raise Body Functioning to Its Peak." *Dong-fang Qigong (Oriental Chi Gong)*, vol. 1, 1986.

"On Strategies for Modernizing Chinese Medicine." Speech at the Seminar on Modernizing Chinese Medicine, March 1986.

"Join Together and Greet the New Scientific Revolution." Speech at a reception for the founding of Chinese Chi Gong Science Research Association, April 30, 1986.

"Establishing the Empirical Study of Chi." *Ziran Zazhi (Nature Magazine)*, May 1986.

"Outline of Chi Gong, Chinese Medicine and EHF." *Qigong yu Kexue (Chi Gong and Science)*, vol. 5, 1986.

Paul Dong and Thomas Raffill

Reports on Human Body Science (Somatic Science)

"Dialectics of Nature, Cognitive Science and Human Potential." *Zhexue Yanjiu* (*Philosophical Research*), vol. 4, 1980.

"We Humans Must Do Deep Research on Our Own Bodies." *Beijing Keji*, July 18, 1980.

"Systems Science, Cognitive Science and Human Body Science." *Ziran Zazhi*, vol. 1, 1981.

"Develop Fundamental Research in Human Body Science." *Ziran Zazhi*, vol. 7, 1981.

"On Human Body Science." Speech at the Conference of Aerospace Medical Engineering Institute, April 4, 1983.

"The Anthropic Principle, Human Body Science and Physiology." *Ziran Zazhi*, vol. 4, 1983.

"Research Prospects for Human Body Science." Speech at the 14th Annual Conference of Aerospace Medical Engineering Institute, Jan. 22, 1985.

"Conduct Research on 'Man' from a Holistic Perspective." Speech at the Conference of Aerospace Medical Engineering Institute, June 17, 1985.

"Visions of Human Body Science Waver Around Us." *Dongfang Qigong*, vol. 2, 1986.

"Use Systems Science Techniques to Study Human Body Science." *Dongfang Qigong*, vol. 3, 1986.

"Strategies for Human Body Science Research." Speech at the Conference of Delegates of Chinese Human Body Science Association, May 26, 1986.

"On Human Potential." Speech at the Conference of Aerospace Medical Engineering Institute, December 29, 1986.

"More on Human Potential." Speech at the Conference of Aerospace Medical Engineering Institute, March 9, 1987.

"Human Potential and an Educational Revolution." Speech at

the 16th Annual Conference of Aerospace Medical Engineering Institute, February 11, 1987.

"Discussion of Human Body Science Research." Speech at the Human Body Science Association, 1987.

"Human Body Science Research in Proper Perspective." Speech at the Conference of Aerospace Medical Engineering Institute, May 25, 1987.

"On the Scope of Human Body Science Research." Speech at the Conference of Aerospace Medical Engineering Institute, June 15, 1987.

"The Large-Scale System Perspective is the Basis for Human Body Science." Speech at the Conference of Aerospace Medical Engineering Institute, June 29, 1987.

"Let Marxist Philosophy Guide Human Body Science Research." Speech at board meeting of Chinese Human Body Science Association, September 25, 1987.

"Human Body Science is a Major Discipline in Modern Science and Technology" (coauthored by Qian Xuesen with Chen Xin), *EHF Gongneng Yanjiu* (*EHF Abilities Research*), vol. 2, 1986.

"The Human Body is a Complex Macrosystem." Speech at the Conference of Aerospace Medical Engineering Institute, April 25, 1988.

The first section above, "Reports on EHF," the second, "Reports on Traditional Chinese Medicine and Chi Gong Theory," and the third, "Reports on Human Body Science," include seventeen research papers and sixteen lectures at conferences. This would not be considered much for an ordinary researcher, but for one laden with many responsibilities, it clearly shows the devotion of a significant amount of time and thought to the development of China's EHF research.

Qian Xuesen believes that to study EHF, we must study

chi gong and Chinese medicine, and the three of them are part of a unified system. Human body science (also called somatic science) is rooted in the fertile soil of these three things. As Qian Xuesen explained, "Our academic organization is called 'Chinese Human Body Science Research Society' above all to clarify the scope of human body science research. Modern science has been divided into nine major disciplines [*author's note:* Dr. Qian refers to natural science, social science, mathematics, systems science, cognitive science, human body science, military science, aesthetics, and behavioral science], and among them human body science is a major field, ranking with natural science and social science in scope. It covers a wide range of issues, but this should be determined empirically. We must not attempt an overly broad research target too quickly. In the coming phase, we should mention EHF as a major focus of research, along with the science of chi gong and the modernization of traditional Chinese medicine."

Dr. Qian has affirmed that the basic idea of human body science is to view the person as a massive system, and an open system in close connection with the whole universe around it. Unifying the macroscopic and the microscopic levels, this idea is also called "the man-universe paradigm." This theory deals with the larger systems of man and the environment, and man and the universe. From this we can see three parts of the man-universe paradigm. The first aspect investigates man as an entity in the universe, the second considers the relationship between the inner workings of the body with the environment, and the third studies the quantum mechanical basis of the man-universe paradigm. This includes quantum measurement, with the effect of the uncertainty principle on perception at the quantum level. At the macro level, the paradigm takes in the principles of traditional Chinese medicine.

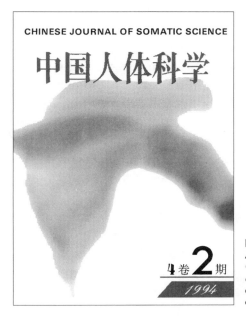

CHINESE JOURNAL OF SOMATIC SCIENCE

中国人体科学

4卷 **2** 期

1994

Fig. 2–3
A quarterly magazine called *Chinese Journal of Somatic Science* is not for sale to the public and may not be sent out of the country.

The philosophy behind human body science has its earlier roots in theories propounded by U.S. physicist Robert H. Dicke in 1961. This was greatly expanded by British astronomer Branden Carter in 1974 and dubbed "the anthropic principle." Qian Xuesen is very interested in this. He views it as "a new field in modern science and technology"—human body science.

Qian Xuesen's ideas are carefully worked out. He states that the human body is an extremely complex macrosystem, a macrosystem open to the outside world and having countless numbers of links to the environment. These include the exchange of matter and energy. System science teaches us that reductionism alone is inadequate to the task of understanding the workings of physical systems of this level of complexity. Reductionism analyzes each level in terms of lower levels, from the human to the subsystems of the body, to the organization of these parts, down to the cells, cell nuclei, and chromosomes, all the way down to the level of molecular biology. ... But we must also understand, from a high-level perspective, the multidimensional structure naturally formed by the macrosystem of the human body, the different functions of each level, the relationship between levels, and so on. Thus, Qian Xuesen wants to combine the reductionist and systems science approaches, integrating them with research on the human body and its environment. These are the tasks of human body science.

As mentioned earlier, research in human body science encompasses chi gong, Chinese medicine, and EHF. Now, let us turn to chi gong research and how Qian Xuesen has promoted it. He considers that research in chi gong must be started by establishing the "empirical study of chi gong." What does this mean? The empirical study of chi gong seeks to describe what it is, but not why it is. In other words, all we know is that chi gong has healing powers, but we don't understand why it works. When we eventually learn why it works, we can raise it to a more scientific level. This implies that the first step is to show that chi gong does indeed work. Next comes the attempt to understand it, proceeding step by step to higher levels, until it can be handled by scientific methods. How can this be accomplished? Dr. Qian's answer is, "By using systems science."

Systems science research on chi gong must aim to work on a number of different levels. The first of these is the observation of the actual effects of chi gong practice. A second is the compiling of chi gong experience, gathering materials on different techniques and publishing them. The third is the compilation and revision of the ancient works on chi gong from the Buddhists, Taoists, and Confucians. (There are large numbers of ancient works on chi gong.) Then we can see if the ancient theories and beliefs conflict with the current practices. If they do conflict, this should be the subject of further research to resolve the areas of conflict. After these issues have been clarified, the next issue would be, Do these contradict the known modern principles, such as those of biology?

Then, after this preparatory work has been completed, a final step would be to do research on how to classify all the techniques developed from experimentation and study, dividing them according to target practitioners by age, sex, lifestyle (such as Oriental versus Western lifestyles), and condition of health (whether sick or weak, and so on).

"Reviewing history," says Dr. Qian, "our ancestors were wild men, with no medicine and no capabilities for curing disease. All they had was their own natural resistance to disease. Later, medicine was discovered, and this began the first stage in the history of medical science. As it developed further, we came to know about immunology. This transition from curing to preventing disease was the second stage in medical science. Now, the medical world has taken up recuperative medicine. This means not only curing and preventing disease, but also restoring the health to a good level of functioning. This is the third stage." However, Qian Xuesen doesn't think it will end here. The next stage will be to raise the health to its highest level of functioning. The practice of chi gong could play a role in this, because chi gong can help people achieve their maximum potential.

Why do the Chinese government and Qian Xuesen take chi gong so seriously? Many mysterious things are wrapped up in this. Besides the health, healing, and longevity benefits of chi gong, it can also improve the mental capacity. The Buddhist texts say, "Stillness gives rise to wisdom." In other words, long practice of chi gong will gradually improve the intellect. One piece of information revealed by Qian Xuesen is that a number of elementary-school teachers in China have been training their students in chi gong. The result was that the children's scores in all subjects went up, particularly in mathematics. This has been confirmed by statistical methods. Delighted, Qian Xuesen has said, "This is a very important thing. The world of the twenty-first century will be a battle-field of knowledge."

As he has pointed out in particular, "Another matter of vital importance is that the facts demonstrate that practicing chi gong gives rise to EHF. This is a task with far-reaching implications. We must exert every effort in this!"

Now, let us turn to Dr. Qian's views on the development of Chinese medicine. On March 4, 1986, at the Scientific Seminar on the Modernization of Chinese Medicine, he presented his talk "On Strategies for the Modernization of Chinese Medicine." In this seminar, he spoke for developing Chinese medicine in a modern direction, first by establishing an "empirical theory of Chinese medicine." An empirical theory is one completely derived from the actual phenomena, forming generalizations and systematic ideas based on them. In other words, as its starting point, it looks at the *what* but not the *why*. It describes the results of experience and places them in an ordered context. This is what is meant by empirical Chinese medical science.

In the last two decades, because Western medicine has been unable to deal with numerous complicated modern diseases, many people advocate going back to nature, seeking the solution through natural healing. For this reason, people from many countries go to China to study Chinese medicine and acupuncture. In this, they are not stopped by the language barrier, but they do encounter a barrier created by the ancient terminology. Indeed, it is not only these foreigners who face such a barrier, even the native Chinese themselves face the same difficulty. An educated Chinese will not necessarily be able to understand the ancient Chinese terms and concepts. "How hard it must be for a foreigner to study the Chinese medicine text, *The Yellow Emperor's Classic of Internal Medicine*," quips Dr. Qian.

Dr. Qian has proposed that the only way to develop Chinese medicine is to use modern scientific systems and terminology, pulling it apart from the ancient methods and philosophies and creating an empirical theory expressed in terms of modern science. In his writings, Qian Xuesen gives an example. In 1973 a foreigner called Goldberg (the report did not give his first name or nationality), and in 1977 China's Professor Kuang Anjing, working independently, showed by analysis of scientific experiments that the Chinese medicine concepts of *yin xu* (deficiency of *yin* or negative principle) and *yang xu* (deficiency of *yang* or positive principle) for diagnosis are at least in some cases directly related to cAMp and cGMp content in the bloodstream. This is a translation of a Chinese medical term into the language of modern science.

As another very good example of this, a researcher in Chinese medicine, Zhang Ruijun, has applied the principles of systems science (Qian Xuesen is a big promoter of systems science) to compare and contrast the Chinese medicine concept of *zheng* ("sign" or "indication") with the Western medicine concept translated in Chinese by *zheng* ("symptom" or "disease"). (The two words are pronounced the same in Chinese but are written with different Chinese characters and have different meanings.) There is a major difference between the two, because the latter refers to concrete symptoms such as headaches, coughs, or vomiting, but the former is a general term for an entire collection of effects appearing at a certain stage in the development of a disease.

Because it implies an analysis and synthesis of the place, cause, and nature of the disease process, "indication" is a more complete concept than "symptom." For this reason, it becomes clear that it leads to more broadly based solutions than merely treating each symptom separately—treating the head for a headache or treating the foot for a foot ache. When Zhang Ruijun speaks of *zheng* (indication), he is referring to the "level of functioning." Qian Xuesen believes that this is the root of the matter.

However, in recent years, some researchers in Chinese and Western medicine have replaced *zheng* (indication) with *zheng* (symptom), believing that "symptoms" are the more important concept. Qian Xuesen believes some Chinese have gone too far in that direction, as in the article "A Comparison and Contrasting of Chinese and Western Ideas on Clinical Practice," published in *Reports of the Shandong Academy of Chinese Medicine* (volume 1, 1986), in which author Liu Shijue was even so bold as to say the Chinese medicine concept of "indication" was unscientific! Dr. Qian said, "From the systems science perspective, the concept of 'indications' in Chinese medicine is entirely scientific." Indications take the form of effects in the functioning of the body. As to why the human body has gone into such a state of functioning, of course there are bacteria, infections, and so on. Thus, Chinese medicine's indications express this on a high level and are fully scientific.

For the modernization of Chinese medicine, Dr. Qian advocates a strategy of systems-level and holistic approaches. He has discussed topics under active research in Western medicine. For example, an article in the October 1985 issue of *Scientific American* played up the achievements of molecular biology, which encapsulated all of life's phenomena under three categories: proteins (including enzymes), DNA and RNA, and of course cells and their membranes. He has said that, unfortunately, this approach is inadequate. This is because the research lacks a high-level or holistic perspective. Qian Xuesen would prefer to act under the guidance of systems science, bringing about a new medical revolution by moving from the micro-level to the level of the whole organism.

As mentioned earlier, chi gong, Chinese medicine, and EHF are three parts of the same system. An approach that can deal with Chinese medicine and chi gong will help the development of EHF research as well. One reason researchers in other countries have not given EHF as much attention as it deserves is the unstable nature of EHF. You cannot make EHF appear on demand. For this reason, it is considered unreliable. Currently, the Chinese are using chi gong and Chinese medicine (including acupuncture) to raise people with EHF to their highest level of functioning (or "eigenstate" in the jargon of systems science), and improve the stability of the abilities.

It is because chi gong is popular in China today that thousands upon thousands of people with EHF have appeared there (Yan Xin is just one of these). There may be as many in China as the rest of the world put together. If a so-called "psychic war" ever takes place, China's opponents face certain defeat. However, the Chinese government has many purposes for pursuing EHF research. Besides the military and security applications, it also has industrial uses (such as for mineral prospecting), medical applications, navigational and policing applications, et cetera. Yao Zheng, the daughter of my friend, is currently using her powers as a guide in exploration for water and oil resources (*see chapter 11*).

The central figure of this chapter, Dr. Qian, has not personally directed EHF research; he has merely proposed the general directions. But everyone has moved forward in these directions. The Chinese respect him for both his intelligence and his talent. Since he has strongly called for theoretical and applied research in chi gong, Chinese medicine, and EHF as three parts of a single system, everyone has been eager to realize the potential of this approach. His support has led people to develop EHF to the degree of the "gods" or spirit beings. What the ancients believed was the work of these spirit beings was one and the same as the EHF of today. The only difference is that the ancients had no idea what it was, but today, we know what it is, and are making great efforts to explain how it works. It is a very important thing, a scientific revolution in the making!

• 3 •

China's Psychic Research: First Stage
(Discovery and Rise to Prominence)

C hina has 5,000 years of recorded history. Why wasn't EHF discovered earlier? Why did it take until 1979 to finally be discovered? It would be a mistake for us to think this way. There are many records of EHF phenomena in the ancient Chinese texts, but in those days it was believed that such people were gods and not men. Some even viewed the phenomena as black magic, and were afraid to get near it and see it for what it was. In his discussions of EHF, Qian Xuesen has also raised this issue. He said, "What the ancients called gods could be people with EHF. They didn't understand what it was at that time, so they called them gods. . . ."

China is not the only country that has made gods out of people. Even some supposedly scientifically advanced countries in the last decade of the twentieth century have mystified these matters in similar ways. After Yan Xin, a top super psychic from China, visited America for two years and returned to China, he told China's *Guofang Qigong Bao* (*National Defense Chi Gong News*) that he did many surprising things with his EHF powers when in the U.S. (*see chapter 6 for a full discussion of this*), but the Americans were afraid to publish stories about them because they thought the news of these almost mystical experiences would cause an uproar. In particular, it would have "subjected the religious community and the philosophical community to the challenge of Yan Xin, and shaken their positions."

Today, we know more than the ancients did, and we have the courage to face these strange things head-on. This is why we have finally discovered that what were called "gods" or "black magic arts" are nothing more than human potentials we all have, but which are more strongly developed in some people than in others. When these potentials are developed, they are known as EHF or psychic powers.

Perhaps 1979 was a lucky year for China. On March 11 of that year, *Sichuan Daily* reported an astonishing news item to the whole country. It said that its reporters, along with the provincial secretary of the Communist Party, Yang Zhao, had discovered that Tang Yu, a twelve-year-old child in Dazu County, Sichuan Province, could read with his ear. When this news spread, it caused an uproar among a large number of the sort of people who try to make men into gods. It also brought strong recriminations from many in the mainstream scientific community. This led to great confusion in the intellectual world.

How was Tang Yu discovered? One day in 1978, Tang Yu was taking a walk with a friend named Chen. Suddenly he said, "Chen, don't you have a pack of Flying Swan cigarettes in your pocket?" Chen answered that he did, and asked how

CHINA'S SUPER PSYCHICS

Fig. 3–1
Two scientists (left and right) testing the EHF of three children. The one in the cap is Tang Yu.

he knew. Tang Yu smiled and didn't reply. After this, on many occasions Tang Yu was found to have the ability to read with his ear. In particular, many of his schoolmates learned of this. This was an amazing story, and the news spread rapidly. Thus, the head editor of *Sichuan Daily*, Li Li, met with reporter Zhang Naiming and told him to go to the village in Dazu County to cover the story of the wonder child Tang Yu who could "read with his ears."

The reporter arrived at Dazu County, did extensive investigations and interviews, and for additional verification went to the neighboring town Jiangjin. He reached the conclusion that there was something to the story. To make a good report for his head editor, Zhang Naiming decided that there is

• 43 •

Paul Dong and Thomas Raffill

nothing like seeing for oneself. He arranged to meet Tang Yu to test him personally, having received permission from the local government authorities to do so.

Early one fine morning, Zhang Naiming invited Tang Yu to his lodging, giving him a test paper he had already prepared and folded six times. As Zhang and the provincial-party secretary Yang Zhao watched Tang Yu intently, he held the test papers by his ear for a little bit, then said, "You wrote the four characters *an ding tuan jie* [stability and unity] in blue ink." His test result was absolutely right!

Of course, they did not test only one time. Each time, they tested with two or three words, or as much as a sentence or two. In one test, they wrote four lines of poetry by the famous classical Chinese poet Li Bo, which Tang Yu also was able to read with his ear. The poem was, *"A patch of moonlight before my bed, I thought it might be frost upon the ground. I looked up at the bright moon, then dropped my head and felt homesick."* If their eyes didn't deceive them, it was all true. Zhang Naiming's report was published. The story was then carried by *Shanghai Science and Technology News, Hubei Science and Technology News, Anhui Science and Technology News,* and several major provincial papers. The story was also broadcast on the "Voice of America."

In the following period, countless numbers of reporters from all over China and official delegations and research teams from nearby regions poured into Dazu County. Naturally, such a sensational incident also became the target of attack by traditional scientists, because "reading with the ear" flies in the face of common sense. For this reason, these scientists and self-appointed intellectuals felt they could "obviously" judge the case a fraud without the need to investigate any facts. They said, "Such a thing as reading with the ear could never be done, except by magicians and frauds!"

Fig. 3-2
The discovery of Tang Yu shook the Chinese media.

In a period of no more than two months, the official publication of the national government and the Communist Party,
and the most important newspaper in China, *People's Daily*,
published an article under the headline, "From Smelling
Words to Reading with the Ear," which snarled that reading
with the nose, ear, or anything like it didn't exist and went
against commonsense scientific principles. After that, no
publications dared to report on these matters. A chill also fell
over the general public's interest in EHF investigation. Following the lead of the *People's Daily*, local newspapers everywhere published a whole series of attack articles, and this put
a further damper on people's enthusiasm.

But how could a new discovery just disappear like that?
One of the great old-time writers in China, Lu Xun, once said,

"Even if a thing is not born in silence, it will die in silence." In the period of silence, some of the staff of the well-known Shanghai magazine *Ziran Zazhi* (*Nature Magazine*) understood that the stories of "reading with the ear" were not made up. They also had gathered plenty of information about other similar EHF children from all parts of China. Therefore, they assigned several reporters to accompany a group of people from the scientific, medical, and educational fields and the news media to Beijing to test the EHF girls Wang Qiang and Wang Bin. They held three tests of these two sisters, and the results showed that their powers were real.

The observers also wanted to know what it was like when Wang Qiang and Wang Bin were reading. The girls said that when they put the writing by their ears, on their noses, or under their armpits, as soon as they felt the print, the words or images appeared in their minds. The words or images would appear only for an instant and disappear again right away. Also, they couldn't tell when these visions would appear, so it took concentrated effort to catch them. That is why test subjects always feel exhausted after such testing. If they couldn't see the vision clearly or put it all to memory the first time it came, they had to wait for it to appear again a second time. For example, one time when Wang Qiang was trying to see an object in her armpit, she could tell it was blue and red, but couldn't distinguish which was inside and which was outside. To see it a second time she had to wait thirty-three minutes. The situation was similar when I tested the EHF lady Yao Zheng in Tianjin (*see chapter 11*).

After the team of investigators headed by *Nature Magazine* had ascertained the facts of the case, they published a detailed account of their three sets of tests in that journal's September issue.

After *Nature Magazine* struck this counterblow against *Peo-*

ple's Daily, an interesting historical item also came to light. As confirmed by He Qingnian of the Beijing Chinese Medicine Research Institute, when Marshal He Long of the Central Military Commission was on a tour of inspection in Guangdong province in 1964, a staff officer in the army told him there was a teenage boy in the local region who could see through walls and other objects. When he first heard this seemingly nonsensical story, his first reaction was disbelief. However, he immediately thought that if it did exist, it would be an excellent tool for the military. For this reason, he decided to see for himself. After the child was summoned, he asked him, "I've heard you have a great ability to see through walls. Can you see what I have in my pocket?" The boy turned his gaze on He Long's pocket, and after concentrating for some time he said, "It is a medical certificate!" On hearing this, He Long roared with laughter and said, "Correct!" He took the medical certificate out of his pocket and showed it to the child. After this, he gave an order to "protect this child!"

He Long is not the only person who met this child, whose name was not revealed for reasons of military secrecy. Zhao Ziyang, who was at that time the Communist Party secretary of Guangdong Province (he later became premier and general party secretary of China, but was stripped of his titles in a political incident), also made an investigation of this boy. He asked the boy to see what was in the next room. He said, "Nothing but ammunition and guns." Zhao Ziyang was totally convinced.

These two events had been kept secret, but now, because these strange EHF stories were being published by *Sichuan Daily* and *Nature Magazine*, these secrets were coming out for the first time. Then, with this basis established, many other newspapers and magazines wrote up investigations of Tang Yu, Wang Qiang and Wang Bin, and other EHF children that proved their powers were true. This ran directly counter to *People's Daily* and its followers. Meanwhile, the National Science Council and Chinese Academy of Sciences were receiving a steady stream of letters of introduction about EHF from all around China. The ranks of the EHF children reached thirty-plus. These EHF children generally ranged from eight to fifteen years of age, although there was one twenty-five-year-old lady named Mu Fengjin.

Actually, a month before the discovery of the EHF children Wang Qiang and Wang Bin, a second-grade schoolgirl named Jiang Yan was discovered in Beijing. One day, Liang Shuwen, an employee of Beijing's Capital Steel Company, was talking with her daughter about the amazing story of Tang Yu in *Sichuan Daily*. To her surprise, Jiang Yan said, "Mommy, I can do it too." Her mother thought she was joking, but she wrote down the figure *0.1* on a piece of paper, folded it up many times, and handed it to Jiang Yan to let her guess. Jiang Yan put it beside her ear, and not long afterward, she recognized the test word, 0.1. Her mother was still doubtful, so she wrote *Down with Jiang Qing.* Perhaps out of fear, she used a different Chinese character for "Jiang" than the one used in "Jiang Qing," Chairman Mao's wife and the leader of the Gang of Four. After Jiang Yan read it, she said, "Mommy, you used the wrong character for 'Jiang'." Her mother was astonished.

A few days later, her mother decided to report this to her school. The principal and teachers conducted tests of Jiang Yan, and she passed all of them. Then they reported this to the local department of education. This department sent a lady to bring the eight-year-old Jiang Yan to the Psychology Institute of the Chinese Academy of Sciences for a series of tests. Over twenty scientific research workers confirmed that this thing was real.

CHINA'S SUPER PSYCHICS

Anhui Keji Bao (*Anhui Science and Technology News*) was just as strong in reporting on EHF children. In its issues of April 6 and 21 it reported that two schoolgirls in Xuancheng Junior High School, Hu Lian and He Xiaoqin, were able to recognize color and read words with their ears. The story was confirmed by the school.

Now, let us step back to ask the question, Why were all of these EHF children reading with their ears, noses, and armpits? Actually, there were also cases of reading with the palms, fingers, and forehead, but since Tang Yu was the first and read with his ear, the other children followed his example, so most of them did the reading with their ears. No matter which part of the body is used for the reading, the operative phrase is *sense perception*. What this means is that when you give a test sample to an EHF child, he or she will sense what it is in the mind. The only difference would be in how much time it takes to perceive it.

An example can illustrate this very well. On May 18, 1982, after Marshal Ye Jianying of the Central Military Commission learned of Zhang Baosheng's EHF, he wanted to see a demonstration. Editor Zhu Yiyi of *Nature Magazine* (she was general secretary of the Planning Committee for the Chinese Exceptional Human Functions Research Association at the time) brought Zhang Baosheng to Marshal Ye's estate in Guangzhou. To start out, Ye had a test paper prepared for Zhang. It had the words *three smiles* written on it and was folded several times. He gave this piece of paper to Zhang Baosheng. Zhang took it, put it in front of his nose, took a whiff of it, and said, "You wrote the words 'three smiles.' It is written in red ink." Marshal Ye delightedly said he was right. Then they did several more tests of reading with the nose. These were all successful.

Marshal Ye asked Zhang Baosheng, "How do you perceive things like this?"

Zhang answered, "When I take a sniff with my nose, my mind reacts to what is on the page." This shows that the whole key is in the mind's reaction, not in the sniffing or placing the text by the ear to read it.

Let us provide here a reference list with names, ages when discovered, sex, and ability for the EHF children discovered in all parts of China in this first stage, from 1979 to 1981.

EHF Boys (total number: thirteen)

Tang Yu—age thirteen; psychic ability: reading and color perception by ear.

Li Yong Hui—age nine; psychic ability: moving objects and breaking twigs by mind power.

Dong Hao Jin—age four; psychic ability: moving objects with the mind.

Xie Chao Hui—age eleven; psychic ability: seeing through human bodies and boxes.

Shen Kegong—age eleven; psychic ability: performing mental arithmetic faster than a calculator.

Wei Rou Yang—age eleven; psychic abilities: clairvoyant vision, reading by ear, magnifying objects by sight, transporting objects by thought.

Dong Chang Jiang—age five; psychic ability: telepathy.

Huang Hong Wu—age twelve; psychic ability: seeing clairvoyantly through human bodies.

Liu Tong—age twenty; psychic abilities: seeing clairvoyantly through human bodies, magnifying objects by sight.

Wang Xiao Dong—age twelve; psychic abilities: clairvoyant vision, breaking twigs by mind power.

Li Cheng Yu—age nine; psychic ability: clairvoyant vision.

CHINA'S SUPER PSYCHICS

Song Ji—age ten; psychic ability: reading by ear and armpit.

Chen Hong Guang—age twelve; psychic abilities: telepathy, seeing through walls.

EHF Girls (total number: twenty-six)

Wang Qiang—age thirteen; psychic abilities: reading and color perception by ear and armpit, telepathy.

Wang Bin—age eleven; psychic abilities: reading and color perception by ear and armpit, telepathy.

Jiang Yan—age nine; psychic abilities: reading by ear and fingertips.

Xu Qian—age fourteen; psychic ability: seeing through walls.

Li Zhong—age thirteen; psychic ability: moving objects and breaking twigs by mind power.

Zhu Jiu—age nine; psychic ability: opening locks and breaking twigs by mind power.

Zhang Lei—age thirteen; psychic abilities: remote viewing, sensing another individual's thoughts, moving objects by mind power.

Yu Rui Hua—age fifteen; psychic abilities: remote viewing, clairvoyant vision.

Zhang Xue Mei—age twelve; psychic ability: reading with fingertips and scalp.

Xiong Jie—age eleven; psychic abilities: transporting objects by mind power, seeing through walls.

Zhao Hong—age twelve; psychic abilities: clairvoyant vision, reading with palms and fingertips.

Mou Feng Bin—age twenty; psychic abilities: clairvoyant vision, remote viewing.

Sun Liping—age twelve; psychic abilities: sending a flower from the garden into a covered cup, clairvoyant vision, moving objects and breaking twigs by mind power.

Li Xiao Yan—age eleven; psychic abilities: clairvoyant vision, reading with ear.

Shao Hongyan—age twelve; psychic abilities: flying a button into the next room, clairvoyant vision, setting watches from a distance, moving objects.

Li Song Mei—age eleven; psychic ability: clairvoyant vision.

Zhao Gui Min—age eleven; psychic ability: sensing another individual's thoughts.

Liu Li Sha—age ten; psychic ability: clairvoyant vision.

Zhang Li—age nine; psychic ability: reading with armpit, ear, palm, fingertips.

Wu Nian Qing—age ten; psychic ability: reading with ear and fingers.

Feng Xia Nu—age seven; psychic ability: performing mental arithmetic faster than a calculator, remote viewing, breaking twigs with mind.

Wang Ming Fang—age ten; psychic abilities: X-ray vision, telescopic vision, making flowers bloom with the mind.

Chen Xin—age ten; psychic ability: clairvoyant vision.

Di Rong—age thirteen; psychic ability: seeing through human bodies.

Zou Hui Ping—age twelve; psychic abilities: telepathy, remote viewing.

Wu Ming—age eleven; psychic abilities: transporting objects by mind power, seeing clairvoyantly through human bodies.

The breakdown by sex in the above list is twenty-six females and thirteen males, so there are thirteen more girls than boys. This reflects a general tendency in China's EHF that there are more females than males. Moreover, to the best of my knowledge, China's top super psychic is a lady, but I don't know her name. She lives a life of secrecy, but her existence is discussed in chapter 11.

CHINA'S SUPER PSYCHICS

Whenever anything happens in mainland China, the people in Hong Kong are the first to get wind of it. This is not just because of Hong Kong's closeness to China and the shared language and people. The main reason is that Hong Kong is an international city and pays great attention to international affairs. When the subject of psychic powers began to heat up in mainland China, a group of four students from Hong Kong went to the mainland as part of an academic exchange, having in view the possibility of learning about the work in EHF there.

They first visited Beijing, where they were told by physics students that EHF had been proven in scientific experiments. These students told their guests that they had concluded that EHF was a normal part of human functioning present to a greater or lesser extent in all people. They also said that the powers were strongest in children, and most of the people found to have EHF have been children.

The following day, they went to Shanghai to visit the offices of *Nature Magazine*. They were met by editor Zhu Yiyi, who arranged for them to meet with Zhang Lei for a demonstration of her powers. Zhu Yiyi told them that Zhang Lei's father first discovered she had EHF when she did remarkably well in guessing hidden cards.

Zhang Lei gave ten demonstrations for the students from Hong Kong. Six of them were complete successes, two were partial successes, and two were failures.

In one of the partial successes, the students wrote the word *tian* (田), meaning "field," on the hidden paper. After six minutes and 24 seconds, she wrote what she saw: 凹 and 凹.

This phenomenon, which has been found in many children in China, is called "nonocular vision" by Chinese scientists. It involves reading with the ear, fingertips, forehead, armpit, foot, or stomach. Children with this ability can see a piece of paper hidden in a box, even if it is folded or cut into small pieces.

As Bei Shizhang, director of the Institute of Biology and Physics of the Chinese Academy of Sciences, wrote, "Ocular vision is better than nonocular vision, but nonocular vision has its peculiar advantage—view expansion. With it, a person can, in his mind, make a twisted or cut-up piece of paper with words on it return to its original shape and become intelligible. The person can also see through metal and plastic to read words on twisted or cut-up pieces of paper. All this cannot be accomplished by normal ocular vision." Bei also discussed some of the further research interests of the Chinese scientists in this phenomenon, including such issues as the transmission and consumption of energy during the process of reading with organs other than the eyes.

The eighth test of Zhang Lei's powers involved remote viewing of a piece of writing. The testers wrote on a slip of paper the first line of a famous Chinese classical poem, "*A patch of moonlight before my bed.*" They folded it up and put it in a tin box. After nine minutes, she was able to read it correctly.

Zhang Lei described her sensations during the process of reading the words in the box. She said parts of the Chinese characters would pop into her mind until she got a complete picture. For example, reading the Chinese character *guang* ("light") in the above poem, she first visualized the top part (⺍), followed by the bottom (兀), which then made the whole character (光). Then the two characters for "bright moon" appeared, and finally the characters for "before the bed." This was the opposite of the order in which the words occur in Chinese.

The four students thought Zhang Lei was a nice girl with

CHINA'S SUPER PSYCHICS

EHF. One of them copied a poem popular among Hong Kong students and presented it to Zhang Lei:

Mountains may fall,
Oceans may go dry,
Friends may forget you,
But never shall I.

But such a sense of friendship and cooperation in science as recounted above would soon be disturbed by controversy, since many scientists thought EHF was a fraud.

• 4 •

China's Psychic Research: Second Stage
(Controversy and Conflict)

W hen we raise the question of belief in EHF, we will find several types of people. One type will absolutely never believe in it, a second type will be inclined to believe in it, a third type will have mixed feelings, a fourth type will think that seeing is believing, and a fifth type will be stubborn and refuse to believe his or her own eyes.

An example of the latter type is the former chairman of the Chinese Science Association, Zhou Peiyuan. The December 1981 edition of *Research Materials on the Investigation of Exceptional Human Functions,* volume 2, contained a report, the gist of which was that Zhou Peiyuan had attended a conference on EHF in Shanghai on September 15, 1981. At the conference, he gave a talk on his thinking about EHF, saying that the EHF stories being spread were false, and that people were not being careful enough about keeping a scientific point of view.

Supposedly, he had seen an EHF demonstration, but some people used this fact to spread the story that he, Zhou Peiyuan, believed in EHF. As a result, the leading newspaper in China, *People's Daily*, called him and asked him if this had really happened. He replied that it had, but he did not believe in these things that violate the laws of nature.

Then Zhou proceeded to explain about the demonstration he saw. He revealed that he had seen four children from Yunnan Province. (He didn't mention if they were boys, girls, or both, but the authors have checked this and found that they were four girls, among whom were Shao Hongyan and Sun Liping, who are discussed in the following chapter.) One of these mouthed some words, and a flower appeared in a cup. The flower was not native to Beijing, and it was trimmed very neatly. He asked, How could a flower come into a cup?

Two others saw the demonstration with Zhou. One was Pei Lisheng and the other was Liu Shuzhou. Both were friends of his. None of them believed in these performances, and he added, "If I can say I want something and it comes to my pocket like that, how will the police do their work?" Then he added that some people wanted to form a nationwide EHF research association. He cautioned against this, saying that the Science Association could not accept EHF research as a part of it, the Science Association must uphold the seriousness of science. . . .

Zhou Peiyuan received a doctorate in 1928 from the California Institute of Technology, and from 1936 to 1937 did research on the theories of relativity, gravitation, and cosmology at Princeton University under Einstein's direction. He has held many research positions in the U.S., Switzerland, and China. His first position on returning to China was president of Beijing University. An old man whose whole career was in mainstream science would hardly be the sort to believe that someone could "mouth some words and a flower would appear in a cup."

However, another scientist of equal repute, Qian Weichang, was different. Qian Weichang is one of China's famous "three Qians." The nickname "three Qians" refers to Qian Xuesen (*see Chapter 2*), Qian Weichang, and Qian Sanqiang, all famous scientists in China. Qian Weichang, a specialist in dynamics, has been the leader of the Chinese Physics Society, Chinese Mechanical Engineering Society, and Chinese Dynamics Society, and a professor in mechanics at Qinghua University. From 1942 to 1946, he worked as a researcher in California Institute of Technology's Advanced Jet Propulsion Center. Along with Professor Mao Yisheng, he also watched the performance of the four children who "moved objects through walls and doors." This was reported in the May 19 issue of *Jucheng Wanbao* (*Metropolitan Evening News*), published in Guangzhou, Guangdong Province, under the headline "Two Qians Discuss EHF." The article stated that Qian Weichang did not believe EHF was fraud, superstition, or magic performance. Rather, he thought it was potentially an important new science.

Qian Weichang described the performance in March 1981 in Beijing by four youngsters from the city of Kunming in Yunnan Province. He tested them personally that time. He pulled a button from his coat, put it on the table, and covered it with his hat. The children then made the button "fly" into the next room. (The article didn't say which child did it, and it may have been all four of them acting together). Qian Weichang said that on a previous occasion he watched a "mystery of mysteries"—a demonstration by five children in Chongqing, Sichuan Province. He believed that EHF is an actual phenomenon, but as to its nature, clearly it could not yet be put on a scientific basis. He described it as a potential science, and said that EHF research could not be completed in only a few years, and it might take decades or centuries. In his opinion, the top priority should not be to try to explain how these phenomena work, but to study how to preserve, develop, and utilize the powers—for example, in prospecting for mineral and water resources or in archeological exploration.

Suddenly, the issue of belief or disbelief in EHF—or put another way, the issue of the truth or falsehood of EHF—was turning into a raging controversy at all levels between two camps in the intellectual and scientific worlds. Over 250 major newspapers and magazines from around the country took part in this debate, including *People's Daily* (Beijing), *Beijing Evening News* (Beijing), *Knowledge Is Power* (Beijing), *Guangming Ribao* (*Daily Light*) (Beijing), *Metropolitan Evening News* (Guangzhou), *Tianjin Daily* (Tianjin), *Nature Magazine* (Shanghai), and many others.

The last mentioned, *Nature Magazine*, played a leading role in this controversy. With a circulation from 40,000 to 50,000, it is well known nationally as a scientific journal and has a position equivalent to England's *Nature*. The first publication mentioned above, *People's Daily*, is the top newspaper in the country and a forum for official government opinion, with a circulation of 12 million. Initially, it opposed EHF research, but it later stopped making any statements on the subject, which could be taken as a kind of tacit approval of the continuing research.

There were also over a hundred scientific research units taking part in the debate and research on the subject, including the prestigious Beijing University, Qinghua University, Beijing High Energy Physics Institute, Shanghai Center for Laser Technology, and Laboratory 507 of the Defense Technology Institute, as well as many medical schools and Chinese medicine research centers. Of course, there were also over half of the country's television and radio stations. With all these arguments, mutual recriminations, and satires, it turned into an unusually spirited debate. From 1979 to 1981, *Nature Magazine* published a series of thirty-eight very serious articles on the subject. A partial list is given below for reference purposes:

"An Investigation of the Use of Non-Visual Organs for Image Perception and the Human Body's Magnetic Induction Mechanism"

"Report on an Investigation of a Special Sensory Mechanism of the Human Body"

"Report on an Investigation of the Ear's Ability to Read and Recognize Colors"

"Report on an Investigation of Tang Yu's Ability to Read and Recognize Colors With the Ear"

"The Decline and Recovery of Jiang Yan's Special Sensory Functions"

"Believe Our Eyes"

"An Investigation of the Mysteries of Life Science"

"Abide by the Truth, Investigate the Truth"

"Attach Importance to EHF Research"

"My Views on Seeing Without the Eyes"

"The Question of the Universality of Special Sensory Functions"

"A Test of Color Perception Without the Use of Visual Organs"

"The Process of Image Formation"

"New Advances in EHF Research"

"More on the Question of the Universality of Special Sensory Functions"

"An Example of Special Human Sensory Functions in Directional Orientation"

"Systems Science, Cognitive Science, and Human Body Science"

"Magnetism and EHF"

"Initial Experimental Results on the Human Body's Capacity to Magnify Objects"

"The Process of Perceiving Multi-Layer Overlapping Objects with Special Human Sensory Functions"

"An Example of Special Human Sensory Functions in Directional Orientation (Part Two)"

"Preliminary Observations on the Mechanical Effects of EHF"

"EHF and Acupuncture Meridian Line Phenomena"

"Preliminary Study of the Characteristics of Sense Transmission through the Meridian Lines of EHF Individuals"

"Start the Development of Basic Research in Human Body Science"

"Review of a Year's EHF Research and Future Prospects"

"Several Experiments on Moving Objects by EHF"

Starting on October 15, 1980, in an effort to open a new front in this battle, *Nature Magazine* began publishing *EHF Report*, whose contents included research results on EHF from around the country, letters from readers, and discussions by experts. This spurred the EHF opponents to make new attacks, and besides *Knowledge Is Power*, which from the start had been the leading journal in the anti-EHF camp, the opposition started publishing *Research Materials on the Investigation of EHF* as a counterweight to *EHF Report*. But the opposition, whose main big gun was Yu Guangyuan, still held as its main stronghold *Knowledge Is Power*. Beginning in October of 1981, Yu Guangyuan published a series of major essays in that journal, ranging from 8,000 to 12,000 words in length. Some of the titles are quite curious, as shown below:

I. The progress of over two years of "reading with ear" stories.
II. These stories are not a new thing, and not unique to our country.
III. The promotion of "exceptional human functions" is a total fraud, and is nothing but fooling people with magic tricks.
IV. Articles exposing and criticizing "reading with ear" stories have not been given a chance to be published.
V. It may help to conduct more tests to reveal the fraud to more people, but it must be a truly scientific experiment.
VI. We should decide the issue on a philosophical basis—oppose the empirical methodology.
VII. It is time to stop promoting these stories—but the stories have their roots and will not disappear immediately.

From the above descriptions, the reader will see the array of forces on the opposing sides: *Nature Magazine* versus *Knowledge Is Power*; *EHF Report* versus *Research Materials on the Investigation of EHF*; Qian Xuesen vs. Yu Guangyuan.

Who, then, is Yu Guangyuan? On what basis could he dare to oppose Qian Xuesen? Yu Guangyuan is an economist, but he also held a position of high authority as the vice chairman of the Chinese Academy of Sciences and vice director of the Academia Sinica's Science and Technology Committee. During this period, he was also an "authority on Mao Zedong thought" and held the position of director of the Institute of Marxism, Leninism, and Mao Zedong Thought. From this authoritative position, he directed the attack on the study of EHF.

Fig. 4–1
The cover of *Nature Magazine*, April 1980, showing fourteen psychic children.
Tang Yu is in the inset.

Knowledge Is Power published Yu's lengthy articles over the course of a year, and they won wide influence. However, they also provoked a backlash—each of his articles drew a large response of critical counterattacks. The main focus of such criticism was that he had not actually done any investigations or research himself. Mao Zedong said, "One who has not studied the facts has no place in a discussion." Yu Guangyuan, a supposed "authority on Mao Zedong thought," had violated this major principle. Probably Yu Guangyuan thought that, as a scholar, he could rely on the teachings of traditional science, and didn't need to do his own investigations and research to form a judgment.

As Yu Guangyuan said in his articles, the eye is used for seeing things, the ear handles the sense of hearing, and the function of the nose is to smell. How could one read by hearing words with the ear or smelling them with the nose? His seven articles were filled with such common knowledge as the basis of his arguments, also accusing the proponents of EHF of using magic tricks to deceive people. He said the defenders of EHF were supporting old-time superstitions, denying scientific truth, and reviving metaphysical idealism.

Such a hackneyed and careless style of attack met with criticism from one of Yu's own students. Yan Zihu, an engineer with Nanjing's Meishan Engineering Control Center, published a piece against him in the February 20, 1982, issue of *EHF Report*, under the title "Further Discussion of EHF Promotion, Also Written for Yu Guangyuan." In an ironic appeal to history, he said that on August 10, 1956, at a conference on genetics in Qingdao, Yu Guangyuan won great applause by saying that discussions of issues should be conducted in a scholarly manner, the pursuit of truth should be objective, and statements should be based on facts.

CHINA'S SUPER PSYCHICS

To further make the point, Yan Zihu also repeated a Japanese fable.

> Two people saw a black object under the ground. One of them said it was a worm, and the other said it was a black bean. The two of them argued about it, and then the black object started crawling. The one who thought it was a worm said it definitely must be a worm, but the one who said it was a bean now claimed it was a crawling bean. Actually, they didn't need to wait for it to start crawling, they only needed to get down and take a close look at it. Then they would see clearly whether it was a bean or a worm right away.

He also wrote, "Professor Yu Guangyuan has been particularly emphatic. When the grounds are insufficient, we should remain calm and should not brand others with the label of metaphysical idealist." And further: "These words of Professor Yu Guangyuan from twenty years ago still have great impact for us today. However, in regard to the debate on exceptional human functions, he has gone against his own words to some extent, in a way that is highly detrimental to the idea of encouraging people to boldly explore the mysteries of science. . . ."

With deliberate emphasis he wrote, "Professor Yu Guangyuan is an elder statesman of science. In my college days, I read many of his works. He is a teacher I have always admired greatly. I have written these words in the spirit that a student has the right to criticize a teacher. I am sure that in the face of the truth and science, Professor Yu will be on the side of upholding the truth and correcting errors."

Another criticism of Yu Guangyuan, from Luo Yufan of Guangdong Province Department of Health, attracted considerable interest. Luo Yufan criticized the manner in which Yu Guangyuan, vice-chairman of the National Science Council, made injudicious statements against EHF to the media without having done any investigation of the matter. He said, "Yu Guangyuan claims that EHF research opens the way to the revival of feudal superstitions. This statement of his is without basis in scientific evidence. If one wishes to deny the existence of reading with the ear, one should do repeated scientific experiments to show this. I wish Yu Guangyuan would take part in future experimentation, then give scientifically supported papers or presentations on their results. People are responsible for the contents of their reports and speeches, and we must not casually criticize this or that."

As Luo Yufan pointed out, Yu Guangyuan never took part in any scientific experimental work. Actually, everybody knew that Yu Guangyuan was relying on his intuition to form his judgments. He was afraid to test them with experimentation. People knew all about this kind of thinking by a scientist who is afraid to put his beliefs to the experimental test. For this reason, Zhang Baosheng once said that if Yu Guangyuan dared to observe a test, Baosheng would replace Yu Guangyuan's lungs with a dog's lungs. Some said that Yu Guangyuan was so frightened he wouldn't go outside after that. Another, more interesting story was that on one occasion, Yu Guangyuan was giving a lecture attacking EHF. Suddenly, his belt loosened, and his pants were about to drop. He quickly picked up his pants and left the podium. True or not, there are two ways of thinking with regard to this joke. One is that it would have been as nothing for Zhang Baosheng's powers to break the belt and loosen Yu's pants. Another is that Zhang Baosheng is known to have a mischievous personality and loves to put people in their place, so maybe someone invented this incident to embarrass Yu Guangyuan. Now, leaving aside such anecdotes, let us return to the debate on EHF.

When the pro-EHF and anti-EHF forces were reaching a fever pitch of debate, some observers from other countries joked, "Maybe they think China can't do without turmoil." Other outsiders kicked the pro-EHF side when it was down, calling EHF "Chinese magic tricks." To hear such criticism coming from foreigners was naturally grating to the Chinese, who have a strong sense of national pride. Some maligned the foreign critics as a "new expeditionary force of foreign invaders." Among the more restrained, some said that the foreigners don't live in China and haven't seen the experiments in EHF. As guests in another country, they were disrespectful to raise trouble over this without reason, but it was excusable. But the same could not be said of the so-called scientists living in China, too lazy to investigate or look at the scientific results. Those were the people who held themselves above it all and deliberately distorted the truth.

Out of the large number of articles criticizing Yu Guangyuan, one of the most valuable was called "Don't Accept Maltreatment of the Budding New Science." The author, Ms. Feng Chun, said that any new scientific discovery goes through a process of germination, sprouting, and budding before it matures. In the first stage, it always gives the impression of being poorly defined, crude, and mysterious. That makes it hard to establish its credibility and get people to take its results seriously. Some people would ridicule it, demonize it, or even brand it as "anti-science" and cut off its funding to stop its promotion, to suppress it and destroy it (this part of her argument was a thinly veiled gibe at Yu Guangyuan, who denied funding to EHF research). She said that these people who maltreat the budding sciences could be called the stepmothers of science.

She went on to say that if the stepmother was an ordinary person, the person could denounce the science and not much harm would be done. But if a person in a position of power became a stepmother, it could be a fearsome thing. History is full of examples of stepmothers of science who maltreat budding theories. Then she gave many examples of this, including the example of Edward Jenner, the country doctor from eighteenth-century England who discovered that vaccination with cowpox prevents smallpox. He wrote up the results of thirty years of research and submitted them to the Royal Society, but was met with rejection and criticism. One newspaper even publicly alleged, "Vaccinating with cowpox causes horns to grow in a person's head!"

I believe Ms. Feng Chun is a scholar of wide knowledge. One of her more vivid paragraphs described the lot of some budding sciences that are born branded as "premature." As soon as they are born, they are misfits in the ranks of science, going against people's common sense. As soon as people are unable to explain something by current theory, they jump on it and beat it down. Then Ms. Feng Chun went on to say that many new sciences await our discovery in the future. If a new science appears with the "premature" label, it may be a mistake from the historic perspective to beat it down.

We particularly enjoy her closing argument. She affirmed that, while Yu Guangyuan criticizes the pro-EHF side as being anti-science, people should be able to judge this for themselves based on the facts. She argued for the importance of the policy of academic freedom, often expressed in Chinese as, "Let a hundred flowers bloom, let a hundred schools of thought contend." By trying to prohibit certain types of research and branding people as anti-science, there is a great danger of suppressing new science. Maybe the one who is putting the "anti-science" label on others will one day have the label of "stepmother" put on his own head.

Because so many EHF children were discovered in China, the majority of them girls, the parents and supporters of these EHF children turned to another force in the struggle. How should we describe this? For example, suppose an EHF child lived next door to you. You would feel more sympathy for her position and want to protect her and speak out for her. Such sympathizers and the parents of EHF children wrote many letters against Yu Guangyuan. For example, one of them wrote a letter to a newspaper saying, "I reported my child's EHF to the local science commission entirely out of patriotic devotion to the nation's scientific advancement. I have no intention of pulling a 'swindle' and no hope of gaining any advantage or political influence from it. Nor is there any danger of restoring feudal superstitions by this. . . . Our child has gone through a great deal of testing and experimentation by scientific researchers. One in Yu Guangyuan's position as vice-chairman of the National Science Council could not be entirely ignorant of this. But he does not look at the research, he does not follow the principle 'Real experience is the only standard of the truth' [a famous statement by China's paramount leader Deng Xiaoping] and try to win the argument by reason. Instead he labels all EHF as 'nonsense' and 'superstition,' suppresses discussion of it and blocks research in it, trying to bash it to death. Wouldn't that make you angry?"

Yu Guangyuan not only angered many parents of EHF children, he also angered scientific researchers, who considered experimentation as the basis of their work. If one has very clearly proven a thing scientifically, who is Yu Guangyuan to come and judge it on his personal impressions and crush people with his power? If this matter was not resolved properly, it would lead to rebellion in the ranks.

Even though Yu Guangyuan was facing nationwide criticism, he didn't feel the least bit of pressure, because at that time the world of science and technology was in his hands. Most people like to support traditional beliefs, and the discovery of EHF did not fit in with this. However, Yu Guangyuan's greatest strength came not from *Knowledge Is Power* or *Research Materials on the Investigation of EHF*, but rather from *People's Daily*, which represented the Communist Party and the central government. This paper denounced EHF from the start and supported Yu's position. In the height of the controversy, this paper and others following its lead often printed anti-EHF reports.

For example, on one occasion *People's Daily* published an article saying that since newspapers publicized a child's "reading with the ear" in March 1979, Beijing and Guangdong, Anhui and Hebei provinces, all reported a series of "discoveries" of similar children, but the stories were all debunked by the Psychology Research Center of the Chinese Academy of Sciences and Sichuan Medical School. In May of the same year, this paper and some others denounced these stories.

In addition, on February 24, 1982, *People's Daily* gave substantial space to a report of a conference held by the Chinese Academy of Sciences. The headline was "Criticize the Research and Promotion of So-Called 'Exceptional Human Functions,' " with the subtitle, "The statements of Li Yuan and Yu Guangyuan in the conference held by the Academy of Sciences." The article said that Chairman and Chief Administrator Li Yuan of the Academy of Sciences and Vice-Chairman Yu Guangyuan of the National Science Commission analyzed the history and scientific issues of EHF, using convincing evidence and reasoning to again criticize the research and promotion of EHF in the last two years.

The news report also said that Comrade Yu Guangyuan cited the January 1981 issue of *Nature Magazine*, which stated that EHF or psychic phenomena belonged to the realm of parapsychology. He expressed the opinion that parapsychology, also called spiritism, is a pseudoscience, because it does not follow the norms of science. For example, any experiment must be repeatable, but even a foreign book on the history of psychology that was neither for nor against EHF (he did not cite the source) said that no parapsychology experiment has ever been repeatable. With regard to this, the report charged that Chinese EHF promoters claim that "it works if you believe," so that only believers in it can successfully carry out experiments.

In the last section of the report, Yu Guangyuan proclaimed that now these promotions of "It works if you believe," have had some bad effects on the national endeavors and the people's lives, and that is why we must insist on an end to these unscientific stories!

The article mentioned that *People's Daily* had criticized EHF as early as May 1979. This refers to the piece called "From Reading With the Nose to Reading With the Ear." I would like to mention this because it provides historical perspective. What I mean is that *People's Daily* at first opposed EHF, but since 1983, it stopped maintaining this critical position and in so doing showed silent acceptance of the existence of EHF. This change from opposition to tacit approval gives very good testimony for the history of this issue.

The author of that *People's Daily* article, Zu Jia, cited a famous story from *Liao Zhai Zhi Yi*, a classic book mostly about ghosts. This story tells of a blind monk who could judge the quality of writings with his nose. The result was that bad writers became famous and good writers fell by the wayside. This was a thinly veiled attack on the modern-day EHF children reading with the ear. He said this went against common sense and was unscientific. But the point Zu Jia emphasized most strongly was that reading with the ear or the nose was a trick arranged by the adults, who invented stories by using the innocence and curiosity of children. He said these so-called EHF children, who were being led by the nose by the adults, would later require a great deal of counseling to return to a normal life. Zu Jia also warned that some researchers and leaders in scientific centers should ask for guidance from scientists when they encounter things they do not understand. If they tried to reach conclusions about things over their heads, they would end up making fools of themselves. For example, if they watched a performance of magic tricks (Zu was referring to reading with the ear), they might surprise everyone by being the first to applaud and praise the "spirit ear," and even go so far as to give an order to provide for the further support of the child.

We don't know who Zu Jia is, but clearly he held an important position in this newspaper. This can be seen from the way he often took on a lecturing tone in his writings. The following is one of his sharper scoldings: "China is a country on a low level of educational development; it has children who do things in an unscientific way. That the public could not understand the 'mystery' in this is only to be expected. . . . In the future, the people, under the central leadership of the Party, will march forward in the direction of scientific attainment. . . . It is all right if some comrades do not know science. They can do the right thing and seek instructions from scientists, turning from amateurs to professionals. But a small number of comrades refuse to do this. They never give up the platform, pretending to understand when they do not."

If we wish to go over this statement of Zu Jia's, I would pay particular attention to two lines. One is "turning from amateurs to professionals," the other is "pretending to understand what they do not." In light of the fact that several years later a large number of researchers performed repeated experiments proving the existence of EHF (see the next chapter, "Experimentation and Study"), Mr. Zu Jia was clearly acting the parts of "pretending to understand" and "amateurs leading professionals."

The story behind this is as follows: About twenty years earlier, a phrase much used abroad to ridicule Chinese politically appointed managers was "amateurs leading professionals." At that time, Qian Xuesen made an angry remark. He said the thing he feared most was the "tiger blocking the road." This "tiger blocking the road" was the "amateurs leading professionals."

The anti-EHF camp's *Research Materials on the Investigation of EHF* was not a large paper, it was little more than a newsletter. It had this appearance in terms of both style and content. It could hardly be compared with *Knowledge Is Power*, let alone *People's Daily*. It was published for the sole purpose of opposing EHF. Thus, if we want to learn the opinions of the opponents of EHF, it is required reading.

As a representative sample of the positions they held all through the controversy, we could take the "editorial commentary" published in the front of the December 10, 1981, issue. The commentary, in paraphrase, said the following: Recently, we have seen the *Proceedings of the Second National Conference on Human Body Science*. It is a real mess. We in the editorial department had a discussion and wrote some comments. This research society specializes in the study of exceptional human functions, for example, remote sensing, seeing through objects, telepathy, psychokinesis . . . poltergeists, and so on. Recently, it has suddenly changed its name to "human body science," but it is nothing but old wine in a new bottle. They are not studying the human body, but still working on the nonexistent phenomena they call EHF. . . .

The reader will no doubt take note that this editorial commentary used the word "poltergeist." They believed that EHF research was nothing but ghost stories!

Thus, Yu continued to write his articles against EHF and ignored criticism of him. He mostly left the defense and counterattack to his followers and supporters. *Research Materials on the Investigation of EHF* published many tough articles on the subject, saying that EHF was magic and it was dangerous to use it for applications such as healing. In particular, they made an attack on Uri Geller, called "The Real Face of Uri Geller."

Uri Geller is a world-famous psychic celebrity who makes his living traveling around the world demonstrating his powers. He is a controversial figure, because some professional magicians and skeptics claim to have debunked him. These skeptics say that he cheats in his demonstrations and everything he does can be duplicated by magic tricks.

"The Real Face of Uri Geller" tried to make something out of this mixed reputation of Geller's, discussing a performance of his in which he put ten aluminum cans on a table with a metal ball hidden in one of them. He was able to locate the ball every time by touching the cans, but what was the explanation for this? The article quoted Uri Geller as saying he contacted beings from outer space to find the ball, something that most people would probably agree is highly unlikely. In the end, it claimed that Geller was able to determine the position of the ball by moving the table slightly. In a demonstration on August 1, 1973, he was not allowed to touch the table, and he immediately lost his ability to find the ball.

The article concluded that Geller was a fraud and his performances should not be taken as evidence for EHF. Then it said it was doubtful as to the status of reading with the ear.

We would agree with the editors to the extent that demonstrations by a professional performer are not scientific experiments and should not be taken as evidence for anything. We do not know whether Geller's powers are real or a fraud. But whatever the case may be, that does nothing to invalidate the evidence of the powers of China's psychic children. Moreover, the failure to perform on certain occasions might be due to many factors, such as emotional pressure. Research on psychic children shows that the state of mood is a major factor in their performance in tests of psychic abilities.

Naturally, Americans had to have their say in this battle over EHF in China as well. In chapter 12, I will discuss this in detail. At this point I would like to mention Professor Cyrus Lee (Li Shaokun) of Edinboro University of Pennsylvania, who played the role of reinforcements from across the ocean. This was reported in the September 30, 1981, issue of *EHF Report*. During the Second National Conference on Exceptional Human Functions, he sent a written declaration from the U.S. to the conference, a paper of about 2,600 words. The letter said that many U.S. scholars, experts, and professors were concerned about Chinese EHF research. What particularly interests me is the brief section on Dr. Lee's own opinions. He said that when a U.S. journalist asked his opinion about Chinese wonder boy Tang Yu "using his ears for his eyes," he made three points: (1) Taking the foundations of philosophy and psychology as the starting point, "substituting the ears for the eyes" is by no means inconceivable. (2)

Paul Dong and Thomas Raffill

From the point of view of journalism and seeking the truth from facts, reports on "substituting the ears for the eyes" have credibility. (3) In terms of science, we need greater understanding and deeper research. I met Professor Lee in San Francisco a few years ago. He is a very nice person and is a gentleman worthy of respect.

• 5 •

China's Psychic Research: Third Stage
(Experimentation and Study)

As mentioned in the previous chapter, over one hundred scientific and academic institutions in China took part in the initial stages of EHF research. Since then this figure has grown rapidly, and at present EHF research laboratories can be found all over China. These include Qinghua University, Beijing High Energy Physics Institute, National Defense Laboratory 507, the Institute of Aerospace Medico-Engineering (Beijing), Beijing Teachers' College, Yunnan University, many academies of Chinese medicine, and newly formed human body science laboratories all over the country. These did a great deal of research and experimentation.

Since the discovery of the wonder child Tang Yu, studies on "perception by non-visual organs" were popular. From January 5 to February 6, 1986, the Guangdong Human Body Science Research Association, Guangzhou College of Chinese Medi-

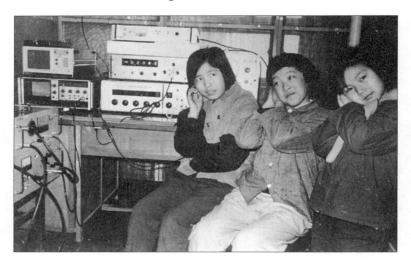

Fig. 5–1
From left to right: Wang Qiang, Wang Tong, and Dong Hao Jin, all of Beijing, experimenting with "ear reading" at the High Energy Physics Institute of the Chinese Academy of Sciences. (photo courtesy of Han Xiao Hua)

cine, Guangzhou Medical Institute, Jinan University's College of Engineering, and Guangzhou University conducted seventeen tests of "perception by non-visual organs" on Ms. Du Ping, age seventeen. The purposes were to gain further evidence of the reality of EHF, and to study the changes in the abilities of EHF children as they grew to maturity.

Du Ping, a resident of Wuhan in Hubei Province, was discovered to have EHF in May 1979. In a test at Wuhan University in September 1980, she recognized forty-three words of Chinese in eighteen minutes. Her rather strong powers are the reason Guangdong Province requested her to be the test subject.

For their test methodology, they used a technique called "feeling the image in a magic bag." A dark blue 45 × 20 cm bag of thick cloth (resembling a magic bag) was prepared.

CHINA'S SUPER PSYCHICS

The cloth was thick enough not to be seen through, and after the test monitors checked the bag, sample objects were placed inside. The test objects put in the bag were previously written texts (sometimes along with postage stamps and pictures). Under the observation of a number of monitors, Du Ping put her hands in the bag, felt the objects with her fingers, and after she recognized them, she wrote her impressions on the blackboard or gave a spoken description of them, leaving the objects in the bag. The results were a success. In seventeen tests, Du Ping was able to recognize 232 words, thirteen stamps, and several pictures. A total of twenty-nine monitors took part in the tests, with the number in each test ranging from three to five.

Huanan Teachers' College and Beijing University have also conducted such research. Their subject was a young lady named Xiao Gang. Over the course of two years, they did forty tests of perception of pictures and colors by nonvisual organs. Starting from February 7, 1982, they tested her powers at regular intervals. They also recorded her menstrual cycles over the two years. They discovered that her powers underwent big changes along with her age and her biological state. From 1979 to early 1982, her powers were rather stable. In 1983, she turned fifteen, and after her first menstruation her powers weakened markedly, and though they showed great variability, the overall trend was gradual decline. Later, they observed similar effects in other girls they studied. Evidently, menstruation had some effect on EHF in females.

In addition, these researchers did a survey of a large number of children (male and female) with EHF. They discovered that, in general, the children would possess strong, fairly stable powers around the ages of ten to thirteen, but after they reached the age of fifteen their powers would gradually weaken. There were also exceptions. Some people maintained their powers into adulthood. This raised questions. Why does the power fade in some people but stay the same in others? Is there a way to preserve the power or make it last longer? Fortunately, they were able to find answers to these questions at a later time. There is indeed a way to preserve the power and even strengthen it. This will be described in chapter 8.

On another occasion, a team of EHF researchers at Yunnan University performed an interesting test on Shao Hongyan and Sun Liping, young girls from the city of Kunming. They placed them in a room and asked them to use mind power to break marked willow branches three meters away outside the room. The result was that in under a minute, Shao Hongyan said the branch was broken. The experimenters went out to check, and the indicated stick was broken. Not long after that, the stick that had been assigned to Sun Liping also broke. Everyone applauded and exclaimed.

The experimenter on the research team then made another request. This time, the target for the experiment was a row of willows six meters away. In about three minutes, the two girls shouted that they were broken. The experimenter went out and saw eight broken pieces. After that, they did another experiment and broke over twenty branches.

Excitedly, the experimenter asked Shao Hongyan and Sun Liping to perform another test. The team of researchers placed a bud of winter jasmine in a china vase and had Sun Liping hold it, but without touching the bud. She was to send her mind power to it. Within a minute, the winter jasmine in the vase was in full bloom. The witnesses to the experiment were all shouting, "Great," and of course the two girls were delighted as well.

Later, the EHF research team from Yunnan University did two other experiments with these two girls. One of them was to make a flower in bloom close up into a bud. At one point, a flower appeared in an empty cup. The most remarkable of the tests was to move a flower into the room from a neighboring room and put it in a vase. It was like magic. The researchers were astounded!

After a large number of EHF children were discovered in China, two documentaries about this were filmed. One, called *Do You Believe It*, was produced by the Beijing Central News Documentary Film Studio, and the other was filmed by the Shanghai Educational Film Studio and was called *Image Recognition by Non-Visual Organs* (about the early stages of EHF work with use of the ear instead of the eye, reading with the fingers, and so on).

In one scene in *Do You Believe It*, the well-known EHF lady Yu Rui Hua gave a middle-aged man an esophagus examination using her ability to see through objects. But Yu Rui Hua couldn't tell the difference between the esophagus and the windpipe, and so she asked the man to drink some water. This allowed her to recognize the esophagus and do her examination. In a little while, she said, "Your esophagus is not like other people's. Other people have a straight tube, but yours goes out a little. There is something sticking out from it." So saying, she traced out the place where the patient was affected. The man was very surprised. It turned out that her see-through vision gave the same results as a medical examination. This see-through vision incident was witnessed and confirmed by a large number of medical personnel and film studio workers.

Of all the many forms of EHF, the ones I like most are making a flower bloom and telepathy. Telepathy is one of the most incredible psychic phenomena. It not only permits communication by thought, even over thousands of miles, it also allows one to know the secrets in the mind of another person. Whatever you think, the mind reader will know—a prospect as fascinating as it is frightening. But there are other, yet more fascinating and frightening things. Chinese science-fiction novels have explored some of the possibilities, such as one story I read of a pair of telepathic sisters. As one sister made love to her boyfriend, the other sister would experience the feeling at the same time, making her very uncomfortable.

It is worth recalling here a scene in the film *Do You Believe It*. Dong Wenbao, a scientist in Huiyong County, Guizhou Province, has a four-and-a-half-year-old son, Dong Chang Jiang, who frequently reads his thoughts. One day, as he was tutoring his son in arithmetic, his son knew the answer instantly. After this, he did the same with multiplication, division, squaring, and square roots. At first, he thought his son was a genius, but then he discovered that his son had telepathic powers. This incident soon came to the attention of various authorities, who sent all kinds of people to test him. Some research units asked the father and son to come for testing together. One of these was the arithmetic equation $2 - 5 = -3$. Dong Wenbao read it and placed his hand on his son's head, and his son immediately wrote the correct solution. Another test was the square root of 3. His son quickly wrote out the answer: 1.7321. He didn't miss anything in the following problems either.

"Hearts communicate instantly by touching the spirit link" is a famous line from classical Chinese poetry to describe the connections between people's minds. If you live in China, you will frequently hear this saying in everyday use. Once, I was holding a chi gong class in Oakland, California. One student was a woman who usually brought her seven- and nine-year-old children with her to class. Once, I asked her if she would object to my testing her children for telepathic powers. After getting her approval, I tested them on the spot. Lightly touching the children's heads with my hands, I thought of a num-

ber. The result was that the seven-year-old correctly guessed the number I was thinking of, 3, and the nine-year-old also guessed correctly when I tested him with the number 5. This was just a simple test, but I found that the two children had telepathic capabilities. I suggested to their mother that I could help them develop their "third eye," but it seems she was unfamiliar with psychic matters, and afraid, so she didn't agree. (Developing children's abilities will be discussed in chapter 9.)

The examples we have looked at so far have all been simple tests. Such tests, conducted on the basis of observational evidence, have been repeated thousands of times. After this, more careful and scientific methods have been used to test EHF. This includes the use of instruments with scientific and medical researchers, chi gong masters, and professional magic performers to monitor the experiments, in order to detect fraud and ensure the correctness of the results.

When people get sick, abnormal objects often appear in the body, such as tumors, gall and kidney stones, and so on, which need to be removed by surgery. Now we have a method better than the most advanced medical techniques. This is the use of the EHF power of psychokinesis to remove the objects from the internal body instead of surgery. Chinese EHF researchers have done an experiment as significant as it is interesting. Anhui Teachers' College and Anhui Wuhu City Third People's Hospital conducted such an experiment, based on this happy prospect, on a live subject.

The target for this operation was a chicken. They chose a strong and healthy chicken weighing about two-and-a-half pounds. They opened up the chicken to place some stones with different-colored markings—red, yellow, blue—in the inner parts of the chicken's stomach and leg, then they stitched the skin together. After this, they tended the chicken for a week. After the surgical scar had healed completely, they started their test.

At the start of the experiment, the researchers told the EHF children Xiao Shi, Xiao Wang, and Xiao Xu (in China, *Xiao*, meaning "little," is often put before the names of children as a kind of nickname) to use their see-through vision to see the colored stones inside the chicken. After the children gave correct answers as to what was inside, they were asked to use mind power to remove the feed from the crop in the chicken's gullet—some grain, peas, and sprouts. After they succeeded at this, the three children's psychic abilities were at their peak. Since their special abilities were now "activated," they could be tried on the more difficult task of moving objects out from the body. On August 26, 1984, under the supervision and observation of eight doctors with Wuhu City Second People's Hospital, the three children succeeded in removing the colored stones from the chicken's stomach and leg by mind power. The EHF psychokinesis "surgery," overcoming spatial obstacles, was a success!

The expression "overcoming spatial obstacles" is not entirely suitable, because it describes the observed result without saying what it actually is. However, since science has not yet found an explanation of its true nature, we are left with this inadequate expression for the time being. In 1982, Beijing Teachers' College, along with twenty-six research organizations and academies and over forty scientists, carried out a series of experiments on "overcoming spatial obstacles." On June 8 of that year, a researcher from that college locked a desk drawer and hid away the key, not telling the EHF subject where the key was. Then they gave Zhang Baosheng an egg (which had identifying marks put on it). After about six minutes, the egg disappeared from Zhang's hand, and he felt that the egg was in the desk drawer. The monitor opened the drawer, and indeed, the egg was in it. A careful inspection revealed that it was the same egg.

Earlier, on December 27, 1980, EHF researchers in Beijing Teachers' College did an experiment in "overcoming spatial obstacles," this time with live targets. They put four fruit flies in a small glass bottle, and put the bottle in the coat pocket of monitor A. He sat in a specified place, and another, monitor B, sat in another part of the room. In addition, four monitors sat facing Zhang Baosheng. The experiment started at 4:44 P.M. and lasted until 5:05. At that point monitor A discovered that he couldn't find the bottle in his pocket. After this, it turned up in a sleeve pocket of monitor B's. They found that the fruit flies were still alive, and they lived three days more after that.

In recent years, the Chinese have done a large number of experiments on the super psychics Zhang Baosheng and Yan Xin. One of the stories of Zhang Baosheng's ability to walk through walls cannot be ignored. But first let me tell a humorous story about the Taoist priests of Laoshan. According to this story, a man went to Laoshan to study how to walk through walls from a Taoist priest. After he learned it, he told his wife that he could say the magic words and walk through walls to take people's things, so they would never have to worry about money again. Then he demonstrated his power to his wife, but unfortunately for him, the magic words didn't work and he banged his head against the wall and was bleeding. I doubt anyone would believe this myth, but the powers of China's super psychic Zhang Baosheng actually do allow the accomplishment of this feat of the Laoshan Taoists, walking through walls.

One day, Zhang Baosheng got married and moved to a new home. Professor Liu Huiyi of Beijing Teachers' College went to visit his new home to offer her congratulations. When Zhang Baosheng saw her from the window, he said, "The gate is locked and can't be opened from inside. Could you help me open it from your side?" So saying, he passed the key to Professor Liu through the window grating. The two of them chatted as Professor Liu worked the lock. But try as she might, the gate would never open (one of Zhang Baosheng's pranks). She kept concentrating on opening the gate, but suddenly, she heard a laugh, and Zhang Baosheng turned up behind Professor Liu. The professor said, "You fooled me again!" This is a story between the two of them, and no witnesses were present to confirm it.

In October of 1982, Professor Wang Pinshan and some others with Liaoning Province Institute of Chinese Medicine tested Zhang Baosheng's ability to get into the auditorium undetected. Zhang Baosheng agreed to "give it a try."

In 1982, Professor Wang Pinshan lived together with Zhang Baosheng for a year to study his EHF. For this test, several professors and a large number of students teamed up to guard all entrances and windows to the auditorium. All of these teachers and students were on the alert and kept their eyes open for Zhang Baosheng. For several minutes, everyone saw that Zhang Baosheng was still outside. After about a quarter of an hour, Zhang Baosheng was in the auditorium, calling out loudly. Everybody crowded into the auditorium to see. Indeed, he was inside. After this story spread, some said Zhang Baosheng could tunnel under the ground, some said he had the power of invisibility, and some said this was a high-class magic trick—that same year, a foreign magician had come to China and performed a "walking through walls" act on the Great Wall of China. When the people asked Zhang Baosheng how he got into the auditorium, he gave a very surprising answer: It was you who weren't able to stop me.

CHINA'S SUPER PSYCHICS

After Zhang Baosheng returned from Liaoning province to Beijing, many military installations became greatly interested in this ability of his, and at least eight tests of it were organized. In one of these, several top military leaders asked Zhang Baosheng to enter a high-government office without letting the two guards at the entrance see him. Zhang Baosheng agreed to "try it." All of the monitors watched every move by Zhang Baosheng, but suddenly, he disappeared and reappeared inside the office. After this, he came out again the same way. The military leaders were quite excited about this.

In order to investigate Zhang Baosheng's ability to walk through walls, the monitors interviewed Professor Song Kongzhi, a specialist who heads research in "the motion of objects beyond space-time." He said, "I have done many experiments with physical objects moving beyond the bounds of space, including many observations of Zhang Baosheng. He can make any object go beyond the bounds of space. There must be some energy involved in this effect. If this energy reaches a certain level, it can allow him to move his body across the bounds of space. This reasoning leads me to believe it may be possible for Zhang Baosheng to walk through walls."

Song Kongzhi plainly appears to be saying that he has tested Zhang Baosheng scientifically and proven that he has this ability, even though he does not admit it directly. Actually, Zhang Baosheng's ability to walk through walls was already an open secret before this. This might be more significant if you compare the previous few paragraphs on experiments involving Zhang Baosheng with the incident described in chapter 1 in which Zhang Baosheng moved a sack of sugar weighing a hundred pounds through the walls of a storehouse.

Professor Song Kongzhi is currently a member of the Chinese Human Body Science Association. He has also written on the basic nature of EHF: "The reason we study the motion of objects beyond the bounds of space is to understand its true nature." As soon as we can understand the basic principles, all other EHF powers may be explainable, including all those of Zhang Baosheng.

Confirmation of Zhang Baosheng's powers by scientists dates back to 1987. In that year, the "Chinese Scientific and Technical Association" held an event in Beijing, and many well-known scientists took part in it. After they saw a demonstration of Zhang Baosheng's EHF, Zhang gained quite a reputation and he became sought after as a subject for experimentation. This workshop was attended by over thirty scientists, and worked on five experimental areas, doing the experiments repeatedly. The categories of the experiments were:

A. perception by nonvisual organs of writing, images, and colors;
B. restoration of broken name cards;
C. psychokinesis (moving objects by mind power);
D. lighting fires by mind power;
E. removing objects from bottles by overcoming spatial obstacles (for example, removing medicine pills from sealed bottles).

Now let us turn to the experiments done on another super psychic, Yan Xin, to see what mysteries they hold.

The main scientific institutes involved in scientific testing of Yan Xin in China are Qinghua University (a school of the same rank as Princeton in the U.S.), the High Energy Physics Institute of the Chinese Academy of Sciences, and many in the chi gong world. Some of the experimental themes have been:

- the body's tolerance for electricity under the effects of chi gong;
- a study of the effects of emitted chi on molecules at a distance of 2,000 kilometers;
- a test of the effects on the half-life of americium 241, by chi sent from the U.S. to China, at a distance of 10,000 kilometers;
- the effect of chi on the counting rate of americium 241 radioactivity;
- the effects of chi on interactions of liquid crystal and fatty matter;
- an investigation of the effects of chi on ultraviolet absorption of nucleic acid solution;
- the effects of remotely emitted chi in separation of gas compounds;
- the effect of emitted chi on the polarized plane of a laser beam;
- an investigation of the effects of chi gong external chi at long distance on bromine-n-hexane replacement reactions;
- an investigation of the effects of chi gong external chi on the phases of liquid crystals and lipids;
- an investigation by laser Raman spectroscopy of biochemically active solutions under the effects of chi gong external chi.

Of these eleven experiments, let us take a look at the first, "the body's tolerance for electricity under the effects of chi gong." On May 15, 1991, Yan Xin gave a demonstration of "the body's tolerance for electricity" before an audience of 1,700 in San Francisco's Masonic Auditorium. Photojournalist Eric Luse of the *San Francisco Chronicle* took a photo of it. The caption by the photo said, "Yan Xin showed his ability to handle electric current during a lecture at the Masonic Auditorium." Before this, at the start of 1986, Li Quanguo, an engineer in Beijing troop 57039, and some assistants worked with Yan Xin to study the effects of electricity. A graduate of a Chinese Medicine Academy, Yan Xin knew nothing of electricity, but he wanted to conduct experiments on touching electricity with his hands. Perhaps the reason he wanted to test this had something to do with using mind power to operate electrical devices like radios, televisions, and on/off switches. It also may have been just natural curiosity. For this reason, Li Quanguo and his team taught Yan Xin some basic knowledge about electricity, then proceeded with the test.

Out of safety considerations, the test of Yan Xin touching electricity started from zero volts, rising gradually. They proceeded easily to 150 volts, but above 150 volts there was a noticeable electrical shock sensation, and he could not surpass this level in many tests. They thought this was probably because of his mental reservations. As all chi gong researchers know, doubts or reservations about something will affect the ability to perform it. A fire walker has told the author that people with mental reservations find it very difficult to walk on fire. Later, Yan Xin did break the 150-volt barrier, and he was also able to make the voltage go up and down. As Yan Xin explained, the master behind him helped him overcome his doubts. At this point, I would like to comment that Chinese chi gong practitioners, the same as Western psychics, often say that there is a master, or a giant, or some kind of power behind them, operating to give them the power. This is believable. The master referred to by Yan Xin must be the supreme master who could appear and disappear, not Master Hai Deng (Yan Xin's chi gong and martial arts trainer, head of Shaolin Monastery Hai Deng).

CHINA'S SUPER PSYCHICS

Why was Yan Xin able to touch an electric current with both hands, but not suffer an electric shock? The reason, of course, is that he used his mind power to enter the chi gong state and create electrical resistance (we will look at chi gong in detail in chapter 8). When a chi gong master uses his energy to control the resistance in the body, he can raise and lower the voltage on the body at will, and also can control the current. Yan Xin has given many demonstrations in China of using his fingers for "electric therapy" instead of needles in the acupuncture points, achieving healing effects by using the electric lines in the hands to stimulate acupuncture points on the patient. He holds a live wire in one hand, and the patient holds the ground wire. With his other hand, he touches the patient's acupuncture points instead of using a needle for healing purposes. He can also use this method to treat several people at once by having a chain of patients hold hands.

According to the experimenters, when Yan Xin is not using his energy, the resistance between his two hands is hundreds of ohms higher than that of an ordinary person. (The difference can be explained as the effect of Yan Xin's daily chi gong practice, compared to ordinary people who don't practice.) When he releases his energy (or uses his psychic ability), his resistance is thousands of ohms higher than that of an ordinary person. The figures above are when he is not being subjected to an electric voltage. When subjected to 220 volts (as supplied by the Chinese municipal electric utilities), ordinary people will produce a resistance in the body around one kilohm, while Yan Xin's will be hundreds of times this. But if he makes use of his psychic ability, his resistance can rise to a level as much as thousands of times higher. (Note that in the U.S., electric utilities generally provide electricity at 110 volts.)

The authors strongly caution readers not to try any experiments touching electricity themselves.

One of the research results could be good news for the entire human race. On January 24, 1987, *Guangming Ribao*, a well-known high-level intellectual newspaper in Beijing, published a report. The headline consisted of three lines. The first was, "Discovery by Qinghua University Chi Gong Research Team"; the next line was "Causing Physiological Change is the Reason for Chi Gong's Healing Power"; and the third, more eye-catching headline was, "The Discovery Means Chi Gong Research Moves from the Cellular Level to the Molecular Level."

First, after the Chinese started to do research on chi gong, they learned that it could cure disease. After this, they discovered that external chi (external chi can also be called psychic ability) has the ability to promote plant growth. These are the sorts of riddles that the Chinese are now attempting to solve, using the knowledge and techniques of modern science. Finally, after much experimentation, they found that external chi has effects on the biochemical level by causing changes in some molecular structures.

At first, under the direction of Lu Zuyin, professor of high-energy physics and biophysics, research was started in 1981 on the effects of external chi. They mostly made use of microwave and thermography apparatus to take measurements of the effects of chi during chi gong practice. Starting in 1985, they started testing with organic liquid crystal and discovered that chi could darken one and brighten another refraction point. This aroused much interest, because cell walls in the body consist of similar high-polymer liquid-crystal substances. This indicates that chi can have effects on the cellular level. But does it? *"Be bold in hypothesizing, be careful in verifying,"* as the Chinese philosopher Dr. Hu Shi once said. Thus, an interdisciplinary team of scientists studying chi gong invited Yan Xin to participate in their experiments. From December 1986 to January 1987, they did seven experiments at different places and from different distances, and all of these gave the anticipated results.

Their experiments involved putting tap water, saline, glucose solution, and methramycin solution—all physiologically active—in tightly sealed bottles and placing these in a dark room, then having Yan Xin send his energy to them from longer or shorter distances. A happy event occurred—the laser Raman spectrum of the tap water now showed a large unknown peak band, showing that it had turned into water of a different molecular structure! This experiment was repeated many times, on December 27 and 31, 1986, and on January 5, 8, 9, 12, 17, 20, and 23, 1987, and in all cases their instruments still showed that large new unknown band. After this, they tested with saline, glucose solution, and methramycin solution, and all of these showed similar changes in their molecular structure!

This is an unprecedented discovery, a new milestone in the history of chi (and psychic) research, one that poses a challenge to modern scientific theory. Chi gong's taint as a superstition thousands of years old was wiped clean, and the charges that chi gong is only a "placebo," "psychological suggestion," or "hypnotism" were refuted decisively.

When Professor Qian Xuesen read of these breakthrough results, he placed a high value on them. In his "Reviewer's Opinion," he wrote, "This is a world first, proving indisputably that the human body can affect external objects without physical contact, changing their molecular states. This is an unprecedented work, and it must be published immediately to announce to all the world this achievement of the Chinese people."

If these technical reports on scientific experiments are too dry and dull for you, perhaps some stories about Yan Xin and these Qinghua University scientists will be more interesting and show other sides of these things. Professor Li Shengping, one of the scientists taking part in these experiments for changing the molecular structure of liquids, told this story. He said this was the first time Yan Xin took part in scientific research, and he was in a very good mood. As soon as he came into the room, he quietly started radiating his energy. At the start of the experiment, the experimenters wanted to turn off the light, but an inexplicable thing happened. No matter how many times everybody tried to turn off the electric switches, the light kept shining. They could not perform the experiment until they turned off the light, so they kept trying with no success. Just as they were about to give up, Yan Xin said, "This should be no problem." He touched the power switch, and suddenly all the lights went out! As Professor Li Shengping said, "This little performance of Yan Xin's reminded us all of the fact that he could heal a person with a comminuted fracture of the shoulder blade in twenty minutes." After this, a lively atmosphere prevailed in the laboratory. Everyone could feel that the day's experiment might bring more results than expected. As it turned out, their first experiment was a success.

The Chinese researchers did not rest on their laurels after they succeeded in using EHF (or chi) to change the molecular structure of water. They proceeded further, and for their next experimental subject they took a cell of an organism. The result was that Yan Xin's psychic ability changed the molecular arrangement of the cell membrane.

If we carry this further, would it not be possible to experiment on those most mysterious cells, the DNA cells that carry the genetic code? The molecular structure of DNA is extremely complex, and the growth and decay, birth and death of proteins are all controlled by DNA. For this reason, our life, health, or sicknesses are all connected with DNA. This is true in particular for hereditary diseases.

DNA and RNA tests make use of ultraviolet spectrometers, because DNA and RNA have distinctive ultraviolet absorption bands in their spectra, called the characteristic bands. These are crucial for identifying DNA and RNA from the band structure of the spectra, in the same way that the fingerprints of people are unique and can be used for identification.

The researchers took DNA from a calf thymus and RNA from yeast as the objects of their experiment. They used a high-resolution ultraviolet spectrometer for measurement, and they had Yan Xin send his energy to them for fifteen minutes. They observed that the ultraviolet absorption spectrum of the DNA solution had indeed changed, meaning the DNA molecular structure had changed as well. However, when the news of this result spread to a physics authority in Qinghua University (who requested anonymity), he did not believe it. He wished to design his own experiment, and only if that succeeded would he accept the result.

Six years earlier, he had brought with him from America something called artificial liquid crystal (MBBA), an extremely stable material. It had never registered any changes. He wanted to test this MBBA. The experimental samples were in the university lab, and they drove seven kilometers to the outskirts of town for the experiment. Then, after sending his energy for only five minutes, Yan Xin said he was done. The authority shook his head in disagreement, saying it was impossible. But when they went back and tested it on their old reliable instrument, the result was there, and it couldn't be denied! At this point, the authority, wittingly or unwittingly, asked Yan Xin, "The MBBA we tested out there changed, but the MBBA refrigerated in the other room won't have been affected, will it?" Yan Xin said, "It might have been." The authority was a little worried on hearing this, and he immediately went into the other room and got the other MBBA sample out of the refrigerator to test it. In twenty minutes, he found that it had been changed as well. This MBBA was an important item for the authority, one he had imported from the U.S. He was quite upset, but some others around him were teasing him about the "great loss." Yan Xin didn't say anything, he just stood there smiling. Eight days later, the MBBA returned to its original state. Some said that such a series of conversions is something modern science is unable to achieve!

The Chinese scientists became bolder and bolder in their experiments with EHF. Now they dared to take on an investigation in chemistry. Could EHF change hydrogen and carbon monoxide to carbon dioxide? According to the principles of chemistry, this reaction requires an air pressure of about 30 atmospheres and a temperature as high as 300 degrees Celsius, as well as the addition of a catalyst. This is a task of a high degree of difficulty. When Yan Xin heard of this, it made him furrow his brow too!

At the start of the experiment, the hydrogen and carbon monoxide were put in a glass container (the pressure was only one atmosphere, and room temperature was 13 degrees Celsius). Yan Xin started emitting his energy, and the container started making a slight noise, as if about to break. Then they replaced it with one of steel, able to withstand high temperatures and a pressure of 250 atmospheres. Again Yan Xin sent out his chi, and the hydrogen and carbon monoxide in the container actually did change to carbon dioxide (it was a little more concentrated than the carbon dioxide naturally occurring in air). The Qinghua University researchers hardly dared to believe this incredible result. A little bit of psychic ability can take the place of tens of atmospheres and hundredes of degrees of heat!

Another experiment was to bombard atomic nuclei. Who would think it? Some say that Yan Xin bends science; here he was bending an atomic nucleus. Professors Lu Zuyin, Zhang Tianbao, Wang Donghai, and Zhu Runsheng of the Chinese Academy of Sciences' High Energy Physics Institute did a test of the effects of Yan Xin's energy on the decay rate of americium 241. Some asked why they would want to do these tests on atomic nuclei. Their reply was, "Now that we have succeeded in doing a series of experiments with EHF on the molecular level, we want to move on to explore on a more fundamental level of matter—the nucleus."

The idea of observing whether or not Yan Xin's EHF powers could influence this hard-to-change property—the decay rate of radioactive atoms—is very appealing. Every radioactive element has its own characteristic decay rate, determined by the interactions in the atomic nucleus. It is generally not affected by any physical or chemical influences from the surrounding environment.

At the outset, they had two samples of americium 241, one to serve as a target of the chi gong energy, the other as a control for purposes of comparison. Each time, Yan Xin sent energy to the target for twenty minutes. These experiments were done six times over a period of half a year, starting in September 1987. Yan Xin sent his energy out a total of forty times. Every time, the experimenters registered a significant effect. Because it is known that radioactive decay is not affected by physical or chemical effects, there were no outside causes that could have resulted in changing the decay rate. But on one occasion, the decay rate changed significantly while Yan Xin was sending energy from 2,000 kilometers away. They had to conclude that the results were stronger at a far distance.

The Chinese researchers became bolder and bolder, or, to put it another way, they became more and more active in testing psychic ability at a distance. After they completed their 2,000-kilometer test with americium 241, they turned to the idea of a new 10,000-kilometer test with americium 241. This idea was based on Yan Xin's trip to the U.S. Using the opportunity of Yan Xin's presence in the U.S. in 1990, Professor Lu Zuyin and Yan Xin agreed to schedule a time that year for Yan Xin to try to send his energy from the U.S. to Beijing, aimed at a sample of americium 241, to see whether he could have an effect on it from 10,000 kilometers away.

In Beijing, four scientists with the High Energy Physics Institute—Lu Zuyin, Zhu Runsheng, Ren Guoxiao, and Hu Kuanghu—made the preparations for the experiment and waited for Yan Xin to make a long-distance telephone call from the opposite side of the Pacific Ocean to confirm the time for the experiment.

Simple logic tells us that if sending energy from seven kilometers works (this was the distance in Yan Xin's first long-distance experiment in mainland China), then it could also be possible from 2,000 kilometers; and if an effect exists at 2,000 kilometers then it also could exist at 10,000 kilometers. To go farther, such as sending energy from the earth to the moon, is a problem for future researchers, and there is no evidence to make any conclusions on this.

As the researchers in Beijing were waiting, the telephone rang, bringing news of the schedule for the experiment. It was decided that Yan Xin would send his energy to the americium 241 on December 9, 1990, from 2:00 to 5:00 P.M. Beijing time.

After 5:00 P.M. on December 9 had passed, the scientists in

CHINA'S SUPER PSYCHICS

Beijing extracted the radioactive americium 241 from the positron physics lab and sent it to laboratory number 3 of the High Energy Physics Institute, seventeen kilometers away. The results showed that there was only a very slight change, and the researchers were not too satisfied.

For this reason, Yan Xin tried this experiment again on June 6, 1991, from 8:00 to 11:00 A.M. and June 7, 8:00 to 11:00 A.M. On the second day (June 7), the americium 241 underwent a massive change of ten percent!

Another type of experiment, designed to measure energy fields, is also very interesting. What we refer to here as an energy field is not of the magnetic fields or gravitational fields in space, but rather the "chi fields" created when Yan Xin or other psychic masters (or chi gong masters) give lectures with emitted chi. When members of the audience at such lectures feel the influence of the chi field, some of them may be cured of their diseases or have their conditions improved, while some people shout or cry, sway or move around, and some people confined to wheelchairs even get up and walk again (such cases are reported in more detail in the next chapter). The scientific community in China thinks these chi fields are strange. Are the effects psychological, or do they come from the chi? To seek the answer to this question, they did some experiments.

Wang Yaolan and Lu Zuyin of the Chinese Academy of Sciences' High Energy Physics Institute have done many such experiments. They invited Yan Xin to give a lecture with emitted chi at the Political Institute in Beijing. Wang Yaolan brought a lithium fluoride [LiF (Mg, Ti)] heat-releasing light detector of a type usually used for measurement of radiation dosage. The idea was to check the indicator to see if it responded to the chi field. The result was that by the end of the three-hour-and-ten-minute lecture with emitted chi, the instrument registered a very strong response to the chi field. In October 1987, they took measurements at four different lectures with emitted chi by Yan Xin, at different places, and also did similar tests on two other chi gong masters. All gave the same result. This shows that chi gong energy fields have an objective reality.

The technique of "field creation" used by chi gong masters for group chi gong practice or healing also has an objective basis. In this "field creation" practice or healing technique, chi gong masters use mind power to compress an area or group of people in some way (or treat them as one person), to gain more access to the immediate environment at that moment. Then the masters send their energy to the entire group, and it is said that they achieve their results more easily in this way. This is a Chinese chi gong technique for using mind power to influence an area, often applied in lectures with emitted chi.

These scientific experiments not only advance our knowledge, they also provide an answer to those who have their heads in the sand and try to deny chi gong and psychic phenomena!

• 6 •

The Miracle Doctor Yan Xin

S everal international psychic celebrities, such as Israel's Uri Geller, India's Sai Baba, America's Anne Gehman, Noreen Renier, and Ingo Swann, have received wide publicity in the news media of Western countries. For example, there once was a British report on the powers of Uri Geller, called "The Man Who Bends Science." However, China's super psychic Yan Xin not only bends science, he bends time and space and atomic nuclei, but the Western media have not given this story the attention it merits. I can only speculate on the reasons for this. Perhaps it is due to a media bias, a relic of Cold War thinking which leads them to focus only on political developments in China. The Communist world as we knew it no longer exists, but Western journalists still only report on power struggles in the Communist Party, human-rights abuses, weapons exports, and so on, while in many cases China's achievements in terms of scientific and medical discoveries, crop improvements, the revival of the best of ancient health techniques, applications in quantum science, or psychic research remain unreported. Such a prejudiced attitude is harmful to the people of China as well as the world.

I first read of psychic research in China in a report in a journal published in Virginia Beach, Virginia, called *A.R.E.* The journal, the official newsletter of an association of the same name, is distributed only to its membership and is unknown to outsiders. There have been other reports in other publications since then, but always in little squibs in the back pages of the newspaper. Professor Marcello Truzzi of Michigan wrote a notable article on China's psychic children for *Omni* magazine. There has been very little else on the subject.

Since then, super psychic Yan Xin has risen to prominence in China. Because he and Zhang Baosheng have such extraordinary abilities, they became famous all over the East Asia–Pacific region within one or two years, and this encouraged the Chinese government to institute a crash program of psychic-war research and invest large amounts of money and manpower in it. They even had a "psychic war" against Japan (as described in chapter 7). However, the leaders of U.S. psychic research seem to turn a blind eye to all these major developments.

On one occasion, I attended a lecture by Dr. Ed May at a lecture hall near the University of California, Berkeley, organized by the California Society for Psychical Research. Japan was the only Asian country he described as making a large investment in psychic research. This implied that Western countries were turning their main attention to Japanese psychic research. I thought of raising my hand and asking him whether this was actually the case, but I changed my mind. Perhaps he didn't want to discuss the Chinese and Russian psychic research. Before the breakup of the Soviet Union, the latter was the main target of U.S. efforts in psychic war. In this way, the lecturer maneuvered Japan, ranked number five or six in psychic research, to the forefront of our attention. Perhaps he did this deliberately, but it is more likely that he simply didn't know anything about China's psychic research, or even held it in disregard. One of America's weaknesses is a kind of hubris with regard to developing nations that leads to underestimation of rivals even long after the situation has started changing.

In the December 5, 1988, issue of *U.S. News and World Report*, in an article called "The Twilight Zone in Washington," Chinese psychics are described in just one little sentence: "In Mongolia, a psychic master lectures before 35,000 people in a football stadium." The "psychic master" mentioned is Yan Xin, but from such a bare-bones report, you'd never know it unless you are an expert in China's psychic research.

Now, I would like to present some little-known but fascinating material to Western readers. In 1977, Yan Xin, a young man known in China as a super psychic, graduated from the College of Traditional Chinese Medicine in Chengdu, China. After his graduation, he started to work at the Chinese Medicine Research Institute in the city of Chongqing. He practiced a method of treatment using mind power instead of drugs. He cured patients of broken bones, diabetes, heart disease, traumatic paralysis, neurosis, rheumatism, hepatitis, cancer, and other conditions. In the past few years, taking advantage of his international tour, he has done experiments on the treatment of AIDS with some success. Unknown to many, the lives of some of China's top national leaders and VIPs have been prolonged by his treatment.

Among these is the famous scientist—"the father of the Chinese A-bomb"—Deng Jiaxian. The Chinese paper *Libera-*

tion Army News has openly lauded him as the "great pioneer of the two bombs" (referring to the A-bomb and the H-bomb). Deng was suffering from the advanced stages of cancer of the rectum. By June 27, 1986, when the hospital announced the critical state of Deng Jiaxian's condition, signaling that his life was almost at its end, all the doctors of the People's Liberation Army had given up all hope of saving him. At that moment, the last hope was to ask for help from Director Zhang Zhenghuan of the Military Technology Commission, since he also served as the head of the Chinese EHF Research Association, to bring Yan Xin to give Deng a healing.

As Zhang Zhenghuan and two doctors drove with Yan Xin to the hospital, they smelled a fragrance, which was getting stronger and stronger. As they were wondering where the fragrance was coming from and talking about it, Yan Xin started laughing. They didn't know why he was laughing, but when they went into Deng Jiaxian's ward, they found that Deng's severe pain had stopped, and he was sitting up. Everyone was very surprised by this. From this, everybody knew that the only thing that could make Deng's critical illness disappear instantly was the power of Yan Xin. In a later discussion about this, Dr. Liu Huamin asked Yan Xin about the laughing in the car. Yan Xin replied that it was simple. "When I send my energy, I sometimes emit a sandalwood scent. After I got in the car, I started sending energy toward the hospital, and I was already relieving some of his symptoms."

There is nothing unusual about emitting scents when sending energy. Tian Ruisheng, a Chinese chi gong master called a "fragrance master," and the over-ninety-year-old Yang Meiqun, are both well known for their ability to emit fragrances. The former came to San Francisco in 1995 to teach the technique to Chinese-American audiences. The latter, Yang Meiqun, is famous for teaching her practice, "wild-goose-style chi gong." Whenever she sends her energy, there is a fragrance.

On June 27, 1986, Yan Xin gave Deng Jiaxian his first healing, and on June 28, Deng Jiaxian felt no pain all day. Until then, he had needed to take pain-killing injections most days. By June 29, Deng's condition improved more. His temperature was normal, his bowel movements were smooth, and most of his pain was gone. He could get up and walk by himself, go to the bathroom, and eat (he had been unable to eat or drink for the past week).

On July 29, Deng suffered a relapse, treatment that afternoon didn't save him, and he passed away. Later, a leader asked Deng's wife, Xu Luxi, for her opinion. She matter-of-factly pointed out, "No matter what people may say, Dr. Yan Xin's psychic powers were effective in stopping the pain." Isn't it miraculous to help someone on the edge of death live another month without pain?

Yan Xin has said, "Early-stage cancer is curable as easily as the common cold. If the patient works with me, I can reduce mid-stage cancer, and control the spread of some late-stage cancer." Ao Dalun, a reporter for the Sichuan Province newspaper *Sichuan Worker*, has covered the Yan Xin story since July 1984. He has many times seen Yan Xin heal people with cancerlike symptoms. One of these was a man named Tang Lao. He was a doctor of Chinese medicine, but he couldn't do anything about a hard lump about the size of an egg on his neck. Several hospitals diagnosed it as "liver cancer metastasis" or "aneurism," but said it couldn't be removed. One day, Tang Lao's whole body turned a yellowish color, he was suffering from constant diarrhea, and he felt exhaustion in his whole body.

Later, he saw Yan Xin, who agreed to give him a healing. As the two of them chatted, Tang Lao gradually began to feel a sensation of an electric current flowing through his whole body. The lump on his neck felt like it was being pulled by a powerful force, and it also felt a little numb and burning, but there was no pain at all. After about half an hour, Yan Xin told him to feel the lump on his neck. He reached out to touch it, but it was gone. Tang Lao could hardly believe it, but he was crying for joy uncontrollably.

Tang Lao is not the only one to have had such an experience, which sounds like something out of a science-fiction novel. For example, on April 27, 1984, Li Ping, a steel worker in Chongqing City, was knocked down by a truck. X rays revealed that both shoulders were fractured, and the right shoulder was dislocated. For a month, Li Ping couldn't move it. On a friend's recommendation, he went to the Chongqing Chinese Medicine Institute to see Yan Xin. He took off the bandages from Li Ping's body and had him lie down. Then, Yan Xin massaged his back. Li Ping later described the feeling as a cool and refreshing stream. After twenty minutes of this, he had recovered completely, and was able to lift fifty-pound objects. Later, according to the X-ray report, the fracture lines were mostly gone, and the right shoulder joint was in its place again!

On April 5, 1982, an employee of Beijing Tractor Company, Song Dianzhang, age fifty-eight, was pinned by a heavy object from a crane and injured in the right ankle. Four years of treatment at Beijing Reservoir Hospital by all kinds of methods were no use. He had to walk with a cane and could not walk for more than fifteen minutes without feeling a numbing pain in his leg. This got worse in the winter. Because he couldn't crouch down, it was difficult for him to relieve himself. He was practically unable to go on with his life. Later, he read an article about Yan Xin in the magazine *Sports Am-*

ateur, so he wrote a letter to him, but without having much hope in it.

On May 30, 1986, he suddenly received a phone call from Yan Xin, making an appointment to give him a healing. Yan Xin asked some questions about his condition, and brought a bowl of water, putting a little salt in it. Yan Xin told him to put both feet in the water, close his eyes and sit quietly. Then he left him there. But about half an hour later, a warmth started moving up his legs, until it covered his whole body. As Song Dianzhang described it, "Usually, I would feel numbing pain in my waist and legs if I sat down for twenty minutes and get pins and needles in my feet. But this time, I was in a kind of waking sleep, and sat there for over two hours without tiring a bit!"

Yan Xin returned two hours later and asked how he was. He said he felt light throughout his body, and so Yan Xin told him to put his shoes on and try walking around a little. Song said, "Then I was about to pick up my cane, but Yan Xin told me I didn't need to. I hardly dared believe I could get up and walk around like this!" After that, the pain went away and his leg returned to normal.

In Western societies, particularly the U.S., many people suffer from diabetes. According to a friend of mine, a practitioner of Chinese medicine, if you compare hepatitis, diabetes, and nephritis, hepatitis is the most serious, and diabetes is second. Liu Tiegang, a thirty-nine-year-old worker from Beijing, had diabetes. His wife was worried sick, and she would often tell people, "I would gladly give everything we have to anyone who can cure my husband." On June 26, 1986, Yan Xin gave him a healing. First, they chatted a little. Yan Xin told him that it was a minor illness and he had nothing to worry about. He told him to drink some water, then gave him a bottle of

Coca-Cola. Liu said excitedly, "Usually people with diabetes don't dare drink this, but I did because he told me to." Then Yan Xin asked him if he drank milk. Yan Xin told him, "Drink three bottles of milk with sugar!" What was the result? Liu Tiegang did as Yan Xin told him to, and drank the milk with sugar. Three days later, he was cured. From then on, he could eat whatever he wanted, including high-sugar grapes, apples, pears, oranges, and bananas, but he never had a relapse of diabetes.

This raises the question, how could Yan Xin have told a person suffering from diabetes to drink Coca-Cola? Wasn't that against common sense in medicine, wouldn't it make the patient worse? No need to fear, because Yan Xin's mind power can change the molecular structure of substances. He could turn Coca-Cola into ordinary water, or even into a medicine beneficial to someone suffering from diabetes. Now let us look at a case in which he changed the structure of white pepper.

Jin Yong lives in Hong Kong and is the founder of the well-known Hong Kong newspaper *Ming Pao*. He has written six best-selling martial arts novels. One day, he went out with the chairman of the Hong Kong Science and Technology Commission, chemistry professor Pan Zongguang, former editor of the newspaper *Ming Pao* A Le, and Yan Xin. Before they ate their meal, Yan Xin took a white-pepper shaker and dumped the contents over his vegetables, covering it with a thick layer. A Le asked him if it was spicy enough. Yan Xin said it wasn't. Yan Xin is from Sichuan Province, and the people of Sichuan love spicy food, so this was nothing to him. Then Yan Xin told the rest of them to dump the white-pepper shaker over their dishes too. This was a great joke. Yan Xin told them to eat. The strange thing was that it didn't taste spicy at all. Even the waiter came and tasted it, and it wasn't spicy to him either!

As to Yan Xin's experiments changing molecular structures, these are described in detail in chapter 5. Today, some in mainland China call Yan Xin a "miracle doctor," and others call him a "new Ji Gong." He can not only cure diseases and change molecular structures, he can also help people confined to wheelchairs to get up and walk again, and people who walk with a cane to throw it away and walk by themselves. Let the facts speak for themselves.

Ji Gong is a household name in China. It is said that there was a Buddhist in ancient China who sailed the seas and lived the life of a wanderer, but he had an incredible power. He gave people healings, never taking a penny for it, and could cure anything, no matter how rare and exotic. He could also create something from nothing, and change the shape and structure of objects. For this reason, people believed he was a god come down to live among the mortals and save them from their misfortunes. Those things the people of that time didn't understand we now know are psychic phenomena. Making something out of nothing and changing the structure of material objects are things known to happen in mainland China today. Indeed, they are the subject of this book, the things done by super psychics Zhang Baosheng, Yan Xin, and perhaps another, greater one.

Yan Xin and Professor Lu Zuyin of the Chinese High Energy Physics Institute were invited by the East-West Academy of Healing Arts to come to the U.S. to participate in the First International Congress of Chi Gong. It was held June 22–24, 1990, at the University of California at Berkeley and was organized by the East-West Academy. Three weeks later, on the evening of July 15, when he gave a lecture with emitted chi at the Fine Arts Theater of San Francisco, the tickets to the lecture were sold out. But Jia Yuane, an eighty-year-old woman, didn't give up. She had been paralyzed and confined to a wheelchair for forty-three years. She said she would be satisfied just to hear Master Yan Xin's voice from outside the door. She had heard of Yan Xin's fame for years. Yan Xin was a miracle doctor, a new Ji Gong, and she wouldn't miss the chance to see him for anything.

When his lecture started, she paid great attention, listening quietly outside the entrance. Yan Xin's voice was brought to her ears by the amplifiers, and every sentence felt like a wave of warmth pouring over her. She swayed and shook to this flow of warmth, and not long thereafter, her waist and legs felt as warm as if they were being roasted by fire, but she also felt that her whole body from top to bottom was being filled with power. The power was getting stronger and stronger, and suddenly, she got out of her wheelchair and stood up! Her daughter-in-law, who was pushing the wheelchair for her, couldn't believe it, and was in a fluster.

"I want to go in," the old woman shouted as she went in the entrance. At this moment, the audience of hundreds looked on her with astonishment. Just as they were all talking about it, Yan Xin hushed them and said, "If she can stand, let her stand. If she can walk, let her walk."

Jia Yuane is not the only person who has got out of her wheelchair and walked again. Two days earlier, the authors attended one of Yan Xin's lectures with emitted chi for the first time. This was at Stanford University, one of the top science schools in the world. Both times, the auditorium was packed. In the three-hour lecture, in which he emitted chi energy, many people were affected by the psychic energy he released as part of his presentation, with reactions including swaying and moving in strange forms. A middle-aged

CHINA'S SUPER PSYCHICS

Fig. 6–1
Yan Xin gives a lecture at Stanford University. The writing on the blackboard says, "Welcome super master Yan Xin to lecture at Stanford." One of the two interpreters seated at Yan Xin's right is a medical student at Stanford.

woman who had been confined to a wheelchair for years got up and walked.

A visiting scholar from what was then West Germany, Professor Maria Biege, who was sitting in front of me, asked me if it was real. I told her that it was indeed, because I myself have a kind of psychic ability known as "empty force" which allows me to knock a person down without physical contact. She appeared skeptical, but later, I met her in her home in Menlo Park (a California town not far from Stanford), along with her friend, Erica Wheeler, who said she was preparing to play for the U.S. Olympic javelin team. I agreed to demonstrate my power to them. They stood one in front of the other, with a mattress behind them (because I was afraid they

Fig. 6–2
The audience of Stanford students and professors listens to Yan Xin with great interest.

might be injured if they fell on the floor), and they fell on the mattress with one wave of my hand, exclaiming that it was "amazing."

After Yan Xin's lecture was over, Professor Lu Zuyin, the scientist from the Beijing High Energy Physics Institute who accompanied Yan Xin to the U.S., followed up on Yan Xin's presentation with a lecture on his scientific experiments on Yan Xin, including the records and results of these experiments. Professor Lu has been involved in long-term collaboration with Beijing's Qinghua University and the Chinese Medicine Research Institute in Chongqing, Sichuan Province. They have been focusing on experiments to test Yan Xin's powers (*some of these are described in detail in chapter 5*).

Before Yan Xin came to the U.S., a friend of mine sent me a videotape of Yan Xin giving a lecture with emitted chi before an audience of 5,000 at Guangzhou Stadium, and I saw the scenes of people getting out of their wheelchairs and walking. But at that time, I didn't believe it.

Yan Xin has given over a hundred lectures with emitted chi in mainland China, Japan, Hong Kong, Singapore, and Thailand. The reason he has turned to this mass healing method is that too many people want to seek healings from him. It is said that the effects of the mass healings are just as good as one-on-one healings, and rely mostly on mind power that he sends to the audience. In his visit to the U.S., Yan Xin spent a month in tests of the effectiveness of chi against AIDS. However, Yan Xin is not licensed to practice medicine in the U.S. and so is not permitted to treat AIDS patients medically. For this reason, the experimenters chose the method of mass healing by lectures with emitted chi. In this way, they avoided the use of the term "medical treatment."

According to Guo Tongxu, the author of the book *Yan Xin in North America—Shaking the World* (Sichuan Education Publishers, 1993), Yan Xin gave three sessions of energy adjustment and healing for a group of AIDS patients from Los Angeles, Chicago, Washington, D.C., and New York on September 2, October 10, and November 14, 1990. Their immune systems were greatly strengthened, and the patients requested a continuation of the program. Thus, the Institute of Chinese Medicine in New York again requested Yan Xin to come into action, an invitation which was accepted by Yan Xin. As Yan Xin later disclosed, he did over ten research projects in the U.S. for preventive treatment of AIDS patients. He used the method of treating the patients without physical contact, combining Chinese medicine, chi gong, and lectures with emitted chi. However, he didn't describe the outcomes.

A report on Yan Xin in the *San Francisco Chronicle* of May 16, 1991, said, "Ken Sancier, a scientist retired from SRI, worked with Yan on the AIDS study, but said he could not release any findings." I am personally familiar with Dr. Sancier, because it was he who organized a class I taught in "Chi Gong for Scientists" (the students were all Ph.D.'s and M.D.'s). I taught them chi gong and attempted to give them an understanding of what chi is through actual practice and facts. Dr. Sancier himself was one of the students. He was not willing to disclose any results of the Yan Xin AIDS study to me either, because he and Yan Xin had a nondisclosure agreement under which nothing could be revealed to the public without the prior approval of each party.

Before this, Yan Xin went to Hong Kong on January 20, 1989, to give a healing to the daughter-in-law of a Hong Kong billionaire. She had suffered a fractured leg bone and a cracked hip bone in a traffic accident. At the same time, he gave two healings for an AIDS patient. One of these was a long-distance healing (or off-site healing). Three days later, the patient's lab results changed from HIV-positive to negative.

Yan Xin does not generally touch his patients. His long-range energy projection has a range of effectiveness from seven to 2,000 kilometers. As Yan Xin was in Hong Kong on this occasion, his long-range projection must have been within thirty kilometers.

In China, from December 1986 to January 1987, Yan Xin took part in seven tests of long-distance energy projection at varying locations and distances. All achieved the anticipated results. Placing bottles of physiological saline, glucose solution, and methramycin solution in a dark room, Yan Xin then projected his energy remotely, from different distances in each test. The tests resulted in the discovery of a new broad band between the characteristic bands of the laser Raman spectrum of the water, showing that it had changed its structure. The saline, glucose, and methramycin all showed significant changes of a similar sort.

From January to March 1983, working with a group of scientists, Yan Xin did thirty-two long-distance experiments, from the cities of Kunming in Yunnan province, Chengdu in Sichuan Province, Guangzhou in Guangdong Province, and Hong Kong, projecting his energy to a laboratory in Beijing, at distances of 1,800 to 2,000 kilometers.

A more surprising experiment took place during Yan Xin's visit to the U.S. Professor Lu Zuyin and Yan Xin arranged to conduct a long-distance experiment across the Pacific Ocean at a distance of 10,000 kilometers. This was done on December 9, 1990, from 2:00 to 5:00 P.M. Beijing Standard Time, and the target of the experiment was an atomic nucleus! (All these experiments are described in greater detail in chapter 5.)

With Yan Xin's EHF, there is one amazing thing after another. On May 15, 1991, at the Masonic Auditorium in San Francisco, he demonstrated his ability to act as a "human electrical conductor" before an audience of 1,700. In his article, *San Francisco Chronicle* reporter Don Lattin described what Yan Xin was showing as "his alleged ability to channel electric current through his body, and his capacity to change wine from light to strong." With the article was a photograph of Yan Xin holding both ends of an electric wire as a lightbulb lit up. The caption read, "Yan Xin showed his ability to handle electric current during a lecture at the Masonic Auditorium." Many Chinese-Americans clipped this article in the *Chronicle*, feeling that Yan Xin had brought them a little glory.

This demonstration as a "human electrical conductor" was not the first for Yan Xin. On the evening of December 11, 1986, in the Central Academy of the Chinese Communist Party, he gave a demonstration of this ability before an audience of 1,200 people after concluding a lecture on chi gong.

Fig. 6–3
Master Yan Xin at his welcome banquet in San Francisco, California. The lady standing to his left is a Chinese doctor/interpreter.

This demonstration was also monitored by an expert. Yan Xin held an electric wire carrying 200 to 240 volts in his left hand, and a ground wire in his right hand. Then he completed an electric circuit with his body for a few minutes. Someone stood by with an electric test pencil to verify that his body was electrified. Not only that, he was also able to raise and lower the voltage with his mind power!

Bi gu (a type of meditation for fasting) is a rare and exotic term not only for Westerners, even most Chinese don't know what it means. *Bi gu* is an ancient term, and can only be found in classical texts. It is not the same as a "hunger strike." Hunger strike is a modern term, and most of us would associate it with political protest or similar matters. Hunger strike refers to the technique of refusing to eat as a way of shocking one's opponents. But in *bi gu* or fasting, a person has no desire for food, not as a symptom of a disease, but in such a way that good health is maintained even without eating. For this reason, some Chinese call *bi gu* "eating the air." The belief behind this is that a person's energy must come from somewhere, and if not from food, it must be from the air. Is it really energy from the sky and the ground, or the surrounding universe, allowing the person to live? Science does not currently have the answer to this. A person in a state of *bi gu* not only goes without eating, but can even cure his or her own diseases. This is called *"bi gu* healing," or healing by fasting.

Western medicine and ordinary natural healing also sometimes use fasting for one, two, or three days as a healing technique, but the Chinese technique of *bi gu* involves fasting for several months or years!

I have personally met Ms. Ha Toi Chun, an entrepreneur from Hong Kong who came to the U.S. on business. She has fasted for six months. She studies chi gong under a master from mainland China, Chen Letian. After practicing chi gong for two weeks, she heard the master mention the meditative fasting phenomenon in chi gong, and since then she hasn't felt like eating. While Chen Letian has been teaching in San Francisco, he asked me to serve as a consultant, and I often meet with him. Three times I had lunch with the two of them, and we ordered many nice dishes, but she never had a bite of it. She would have no reason to fool me, because she doesn't need anything from me. She told me she had a stomach disease and often suffered from headaches, insomnia, and lack of energy, but since she has been fasting, all of these problems have disappeared, and she is feeling much better than before. She doesn't want to eat, but she drinks a little water sometimes. She has lost twenty pounds. The remarkable powers of the master Chen Letian are described more fully in chapter 11.

On October 3, 1987, Ms. Xu Xiaosheng, who had lived in Beijing for all of her twenty-one years, took part in a lecture with emitted chi by Yan Xin. After that, she didn't feel like eating. She didn't see anything surprising in this, because she knew it could be the meditative fasting phenomenon. She was still full of energy, so she didn't worry about it and went on for 133 days like that. During this period, she wrote the following.

> The smell of rice would make me feel sick to my stomach and very uncomfortable. After two hours of teaching [authors' note: perhaps she is a schoolteacher] and taking care of other tasks, I used to need a drink of water as soon as I got home, but on this day, there was no dryness in the mouth and I didn't need water. I felt as though I didn't need any of the things to eat or drink in the world.

Over the 133 days of her fasting, her weight did not go down. This does not contradict the above case of the woman who lost twenty pounds. During this type of fasting, some people lose weight and others do not. In order to study this phenomenon, the Human Body Science Laboratory of Beijing Teachers' College decided to follow and observe her, keeping her under observation day and night for fifteen days. It was indeed true that she ate nothing, but still had the energy and strength of a normal person.

Bi gu is not only found in many ancient Chinese chronicles, it can also be found in *Ci Hai* (*Sea of Words*), a standard modern dictionary of the Chinese language. In an event that brought great attention to *bi gu*, two major chi gong documents were discovered in 1973 in an excavation in grave 3, Mawang mound, Changsha City, Hunan Province. One of these was called *Bi Gu Shi Wu Fa* (*Diet Technique of Bi Gu*). According to a study of the text by chi gong researcher Qian Junsheng, in ancient times, there were three ways in which *bi gu* was practiced: (a) eating nothing at all and not drinking water during *bi gu*; (b) drinking water and eating some fruits or medicines; (c) drinking nothing but water, and consuming nothing else. As Mr. Qian said, the holistic view of man and nature is the general picture left to us by the ancients, but we are still unable to elucidate in full detail all the complexities of this lifestyle. Such life phenomena as meditative fasting, the same as EHF, are yet a mystery. . . .

One might ask, What is Yan Xin's greatest power? I don't have an answer to this question. To give some idea of the scope of his powers, here is a story about psychokinesis, or moving objects with mind power.

Over his career, Yan Xin has done healings for thousands of people, relieving their pain, but some say it is "coincidence," or no more than a "placebo effect" or even a "fraud." His opponents include scientists (some of whom have not actually done any research to investigate the claims). Once, someone registered a complaint against Yan Xin with the Chongqing Municipal Health Department, accusing him of spreading "feudal superstitions" and requesting that his license to issue prescriptions be revoked. After an investigation, the Chongqing City government certified that there was no mistake in the records of Yan Xin's successful cases, but the investigators wanted to test his powers in person as well. Yan Xin told the municipal inspector, Zeng Youzhi, to stand facing the wall, while he stood a few meters away. When he raised his hands and pushed forward, Zeng Youzhi was pushed into the wall, and when Yan Xin pulled his hands backward, Zeng Youzhi started falling backward, until he was so frightened, he shouted for Yan Xin to stop!

I am firmly convinced of the truth of this report, because I myself have mastered a form of chi gong called empty force, in which it is possible to knock down an opponent without physical contact. My book about this, *Empty Force*, has been published in the U.S. and England. The U.S. martial arts world, particularly in California, knows of the existence of the empty force, because in the last few years, two empty-force masters from mainland China have come to teach their arts in the cities of San Francisco and Berkeley.

There are so many stories about Yan Xin, and some of the ones described in chapter 5 and chapter 7 may be more amazing than the ones in this chapter. However, one news item, which I have been unable to confirm, states that it has been reported that he has done experiments on bringing dead animals back to life (India's Sai Baba is said to have brought dead humans back to life as well). This was stunning for the scientists.

To conclude on a lighter note, a reporter once interviewed Yan Xin about his two-week chi gong class in San Diego, California, in which twenty-six of the eighty-three students were reported to enter the meditative fasting state. The reporter said that if he promoted meditative fasting as a weight-loss program, it would be very popular in the U.S. Yan Xin replied, "If you promote fasting in America, you will make enemies in the food industry. They make their living selling hamburgers."

• 7 •

The First Psychic War
Between China and Japan

The term "psychic war" was often mentioned before the dissolution of the Soviet Union, but people did not know what its methods of fighting involved. Would it be to project the fighting power across the oceans, or would it be used at close range to cause a military commander on the battlefield to spurt blood from the nose and mouth? Some time ago, some magazines reported that the Soviets had used group mind power to sink a submarine. If a country sent a team of well-trained psychic spies (particularly woman spies) to an enemy country for sabotage and dirty tricks, it could be a terrifying nightmare. If EHF can stop a frog's heart from beating, it could also be directed against the commander-in-chief of a country's armed services (such as a king, president, or chairman) to stop the leader's heart from beating.

But we have nothing to worry about. The strategic planners are not so dumb. If the president dies, we still have the vice president, if the vice president dies, we still have the Speaker of the House, and beyond that the Secretary of Defense, the Chairman of the Joint Chiefs of Staff, and so on down the line. Not all of them could die at once. What is more worrisome is that the opposing country could play a great joke and use mind power to make the president go running in the streets barking like a dog and the vice president go meowing like a cat. Then the country could not go into battle in the first place. This would fit a famous line in China's ancient classic of military science, *Sun-Tzu's Art of War*: "The best strategy is to weaken the enemy's troops without fighting oneself."

The above is just speculation about something which we hope does not come to pass. However, a decade ago, a close-range psychic war did take place between China and Japan. After news of this war leaked, it was reported in newspapers and magazines in mainland China, Hong Kong, and Taiwan. However, the story has been ignored by the media in other countries. Whether the story was deliberately suppressed, overlooked, or underrated in importance, let us now discuss the causes and results of this China–Japan struggle.

It was November 1986, and Yan Xin was visiting Japan with a friendship delegation from the Chinese Chi Gong Scientific Research Association. The delegation consisted of seven people, and the leader was Zhang Zhenghuan, the chairman of the Chinese Human Body Science Association as well as the Chinese Chi Gong Scientific Research Association. However, his more important position was as head of the National Defense Science Commission, the leader of military research. China's nuclear test detonations and long-range missile launchings all came under his purview. He has also been a powerful associate of Qian Xuesen in the field of EHF research.

CHINA'S SUPER PSYCHICS

Zhang Zhenghuan is directly in charge of all EHF people. In one video on Zhang Baosheng, Baosheng was shown successfully demonstrating his powers of removing medicine pills from a bottle and other skills with great success. But then, in an attempt to set fire to a piece of clothing with his finger, he was unable to make the fire come and looked very upset. At that moment, Zhang Zhenghuan, seeing that he didn't look well, came out, sat beside him, patted him on the shoulder, and said some consoling words to him. In a little while, Zhang Baosheng's finger suddenly lit up and he burned the piece of clothing right away. This type of psychological support from his leader made it easier to enter the psychic state.

On this visit to Japan, Zhang Zhenghuan was not only the delegation leader, but also the director of planning. The seven of them went to the New Otani Hotel in Tokyo. That evening, they were hosted by Furuoka Katsu, the chairman of the Japanese Chi Gong Science Association, and many members and followers of this organization, and, of course, some diplomatic officials and representatives of Japan's martial arts world. Before the start of the banquet, Furuoka complained to Zhang Zhenghuan:

"Just as the Chinese proverb says, 'A barber needs someone else to cut his hair.' Even though I am a chi gong master, I can't do anything about my own injured ligament in my old elbow joint that has been bothering me for many years. Many doctors have not been able to help me with this."

Zhang Zhenghuan realized that Furuoka's real intention was to test Yan Xin's powers, so he said:

"Yan Xin, please offer five glasses in toast to Mr. Furuoka's health." Zhang didn't mention the healing, only giving a toast. Yan Xin understood his meaning, so he poured a glass of rice wine and passed it to Furuoka, saying, "Mr. Furuoka, to your health."

A toast is just what Furuoka usually wanted to hear, because he had a reputation as a "strong drinker" and would usually drink wine as if it were water. He could drink all day without getting drunk, so he happily accepted the glass and drank it down in one gulp. At this time, Yan Xin was about to pour a second glass, but Furuoka started muttering:

"How strange. I seem to be feeling a little drunk."

At this, his Japanese friends all around him had looks of surprise on their faces, but none of them believed such a thing could happen. This "strong drinker" had a reputation for "drinking a thousand glasses without getting drunk." No matter how strong Yan Xin's powers were, they could not be enough to make Furuoka drunk after only one glass. As they were discussing this among themselves, Furuoka suggested that they change to beer for the second glass, regardless of his reputation as a "strong drinker."

Yan Xin agreed to this, and poured a second glass, using beer this time. Although Furuoka was mostly drunk by this time, he still had some of his senses, and he made another suggestion: he would drink the glass of beer in four gulps, each one counting as a toast.

Yan Xin agreed to his suggestion, and so Furuoka drank a quarter of a glass of beer. In an instant, his whole face turned red, and he raised his arms and shook himself vigorously a few times, saying, "I don't feel any pain from my disease now. This is amazing. Yan Xin's powers are tremendous."

As it turned out, when Yan Xin toasted him, he had sent his energy to the rice wine and the beer. He was not only able to make a strong drinker almost completely drunk, but was also able to change the drinks into a medicine to treat his hard-to-cure disease.

CHINA'S SUPER PSYCHICS

The Japanese people have the courage to admit defeat, as well as the fortitude never to give up. At this time, a high Japanese chi gong master named Kobayashi Yasuyuki saw that Furuoka was giving a poor impression of the Japanese people, so he immediately said he wanted to test his chi against Yan Xin's. The interpreter at this time was a friend of mine, Mr. Yan Hai, an editor with Beijing's *People's Sports Publishers*. He felt the manner was too rude to translate, so he rendered it in Chinese as something more like "an exchange of ideas."

Kobayashi Yasuyuki had his own skills to give him the courage to challenge Yan Xin. He is very famous in Japan and has strong powers, particularly in projecting his energy at acupuncture points. He had never been defeated in his career, and even though Yan Xin was famous, he had no fear of him. Thus, he gathered his chi around the *dan tian* acupuncture point (the center of the body's energy in chi gong theory), and made a fierce attack on Yan Xin. Yan Xin acted as though nothing had happened, in the same way he usually behaved when chatting with people at the same time as giving them healings. However, Kobayashi perceived that there was some kind of power surrounding Yan Xin, so he immediately strengthened his attack on Yan Xin. Still he couldn't break through Yan Xin's protective cover, and Yan Xin was still sitting motionless.

Kobayashi saw there was something strange about this, so he stopped and regrouped his energies. He made a new request of Yan Xin, wanting to try to attack him from behind. His idea was that Yan Xin may have strong chi in the front, but he must have a weak spot in back. After this was translated, Yan Xin nodded his agreement. Kobayashi Yasuyuki again sent his chi out to attack, aiming strong power at Yan Xin's back. But still he couldn't make the slightest impression on Yan Xin. Kobayashi felt that Yan Xin had some kind of force protecting his back, so all attacks were useless!

At this moment, Kobayashi Yasuyuki was becoming frustrated. He couldn't attack Yan Xin from either the front or from behind. Could it be a matter of distance? He immediately decided to come two steps closer, raised his hand and sent his striking power toward Yan Xin's back, but Yan Xin still did not react, so Kobayashi again raised his hands to push all his power at Yan Xin's back, but it was like trying to push a massive stone. Kobayashi was so tired he was puffing and sweating. Having exhausted his powers, Kobayashi realized that he had met his match. If he relied on chi and energy, he would be sure to "lose." And so, going against the traditional rules of sportsmanship for martial arts contests, he decided to try another tactic without warning his opponent. He made use of his techniques for attacking the acupuncture points, aiming at the *bai hui* acupuncture point on Yan Xin's forehead. If he succeeded at this, his target would become as stiff as a board and lose consciousness. But still Yan Xin did not move. He let his attacker try all kinds of techniques to attack his acupuncture points, but none of them could hurt him.

Kobayashi Yasuyuki is known as one of Japan's top masters. Besides the abilities to use chi and *jing* (sudden striking energy), and to affect the acupuncture points of his targets, he has another, most ferocious technique. This is to grab the jugular vein of his opponent. When he does this, his opponent may be severely injured or killed. Since Kobayashi saw he was losing the contest, and losing badly in a way he never imagined possible, he suddenly had a terrible thought. Without regard for sportsmanship or appearances, he immediately stretched out his arm to try to grab Yan Xin's jugular. But once again, his efforts came to nothing, because Yan Xin had already closed all his acupuncture points. When Kobayashi made his grab for Yan Xin's jugular, the people viewing the scene watched with bated breath. But Yan Xin just let him claw away all he wanted, without showing the slightest sign of anxiety.

Although Kobayashi Yasuyuki used rough tactics and didn't play by the rules in this China–Japan battle, he was a frank and straightforward person. Convinced that he was no match for Yan Xin, he admitted defeat with a bow. He freely admitted, "Chinese martial arts are great! I admire them." Then he and his son, who was at his side, said Yan Xin was their master and they wanted to learn from him.

Originally, a Japanese fist fighter and a kendo master were waiting after Kobayashi, also hoping for a chance to "exchange ideas" by testing their skills against Yan Xin, but seeing their colleague lose so ignominiously, they decided to avoid further humiliation and gave up the idea.

After the group of seven returned home from Japan, over a hundred newspapers and magazines reported the story of Yan Xin's victory over the Japanese masters in Tokyo under many different headlines, including "Battle of the Chinese and Japanese Chi Gong Masters in Tokyo," "A Decisive Result in the China–Japan War," "Battle in Tokyo," "EHF War between China and Japan," "Legend Yan Xin's True Story," "Pride Comes Before a Fall in Tokyo Battle," and many others.

In this China–Japan battle, we can get an idea of the high regard the Chinese have for the martial arts code of conduct. They will respond to a challenge, but will never provoke a fight themselves. A proverb in Chinese martial arts says, "A *real master does not reveal his power."* The truly supreme masters are usually humble and courteous. They are deeply aware of the ancient lessons, *"There are people above people, and there are Heavens beyond Heaven,"* and *"Pride comes before a fall."*

• 8 •

Connections Between Chi Gong and Psychic Phenomena

Years ago, I thought psychic abilities were inborn. After many years of study, I have come to realize that there are many ways a person could come to have psychic abilities, besides being born with them. For example:

- *Induction:* Hypnotic suggestion or other methods, including the use of words, pictures, gestures, or thought by a chi gong master or other master to induce the development of the powers.
- *Faith:* Psychic phenomena often come along with religious beliefs.
- *Development of powers after recovering from a sickness:* Ms. Zhao Qunxue, regarded as a "national treasure" in China, is an example of this case. She suffered from a serious disease and became deranged. After she recovered, she had EHF. We will discuss this in detail in chapter 11.

- *Development through accidents:* For example, a person may develop the powers after being struck by lightning, being affected by a meteorite, suffering trauma from an injury, or being shocked by a great fire.

- *Spread through chi or energy fields:* This could happen if your child often comes into contact with children with EHF, or if a chi gong master sends you the power through external chi, or if you attend a chi gong master's lecture with emitted chi and receive the power from the energy field.

- *Development through constant hunger:* Speaking historically, China and India have had the greatest number of psychics, but this is not only because of their larger populations. Another reason is the widespread starvation experienced by their people in certain periods. Similarly, those who enter a state of *bi gu* (fasting) through chi gong practice develop third-eye capabilities most easily.

- *Development through practice of chi gong:* This is one of the major sources of people with EHF. It is also the reason Professor Qian Xuesen focused on chi gong and EHF. This is the general trend in China's psychic research. At present, not counting natural-born psychics or those whose powers were induced by other methods, there are about 20,000 to 30,000 people in mainland China who developed EHF through chi gong practice. This is second only to the number who gained powers by induction. Since the method of induction is only effective with children ages six through ten (the phenomenon does not last into adulthood), there are about 5,000 or 6,000 such children in China today.

What, then, is chi gong? Before we go into a discussion of this, let us talk about some Chinese concepts related to *chi*, so the reader will not be confused about technical terms in the further explanations. The Chinese have many interpretations of "chi." In the most widespread use, in everyday life, chi refers to the air we breathe. In terms of the body, it refers to energy, and in terms of life it refers to vitality. When talking of activity, it refers to abilities. In other words, its meaning depends on the context. The term *chi gong* in itself means training the body's abilities, bringing them to their optimal level.

Chi gong has 3,000 years of history in China. It was always used by the ancients for health, healing, and longevity. Its powers also include the development of the latent potentials of the body. Chi gong also evolved into a technique for strengthening martial arts abilities. Martial arts practitioners had to learn chi gong first to give them a solid base of energy with which to face their opponents and defend themselves. Regrettably, modern practitioners are impatient to pursue their advantage directly and have neglected this aspect. Moreover, chi gong demands extraordinary patience and a great deal of time. For this reason, few people are able to master it. Besides, as the economic demands of society became more complex, people became busy making their living, and this practice was gradually abandoned and forgotten by the people.

It was not until 1979 that a coincidental opportunity presented itself for the Chinese medical world to realize that chi gong has a very high medical value. For many chronic diseases that modern medicine has no way of treating, a patient may recover by practicing chi gong. By early 1979, the Chinese researchers had discovered that chi gong is a catalyst for EHF, and also found many people who had developed psychic powers through practicing chi gong. For this reason, they coined a new term, "extraordinary human body functions," which has since come into wide use. It was by practicing chi gong that China's super psychic Yan Xin developed his powers (another super psychic, Zhang Baosheng, has natural-born

Paul Dong and Thomas Raffill

Fig. 8-1
The invisible energy (chi) from Paul Dong penetrates a line of students at the San Francisco College of Acupuncture.

powers). Among the large number of China's psychics today, at least 80 percent of them developed the power through chi gong practice and induction.

Generally speaking, about one in every million people is born with psychic powers. China, with its population of 1.2 billion people, would have 1,200 psychics. Besides, there are 20 million people in China practicing chi gong, and about one to three people out of every thousand who practice chi gong will develop EHF. In this way, China has increased the ranks of its psychics to slightly less than the total for the rest of the world combined. If a psychic world war broke out today, China would clearly be the winner. Psychic ability can be used for military purposes in many ways, particularly for espionage. Many devices considered to be high-technology

Fig. 8–2
A group of Paul Dong's students at the San Francisco College of Acupuncture. Top, Students doing sitting meditation. Bottom, Spontaneous movements by students who feel the chi energy.

weapons may become nonfunctioning shells under the influence of psychic abilities.

Not only can it stimulate the latent potentials of the body to resist disease and develop psychic abilities, daily practice of chi gong can also help maintain the stability of psychic powers. I have heard a U.S. psychic researcher complain that attempts to apply psychic abilities, particularly in military use, are "doomed to failure." The main reason is the instability of its functioning. It works very well when you don't want it to, and when you want it or need it urgently, nothing comes. This is the weak point of psychic phenomena, but one which can be remedied, just as a left-handed person can gradually learn to use the right hand, and a stutterer can learn normal speech.

Practicing chi gong can not only raise EHF to its highest state, it can also stabilize it for applications. As mentioned in chapter 2, Professor Qian Xuesen stated clearly that "chi gong can give rise to EHF. The implications are far-reaching, and we must work on this task energetically." He has constantly emphasized, "Chi gong can raise a person to the highest functioning state." It is only because the people outside China are not very familiar with chi gong and its use to strengthen EHF, or even completely ignorant of chi gong, that they believe "psychic phenomena are impractical."

Readers who do not know what chi gong is may find reference books on it in bookstores. My book published in 1990, *Chi Gong—The Ancient Chinese Way to Health* (Marlowe and Company), provides an introduction to the subject with detailed reports, and *Empty Force*, published in 1996 in the U.S., England, Australia, and Canada by Element Books, gives a further introduction to my thoughts on chi gong. Both can serve as references on the subject. The rise of chi gong in China has helped the country control the costs of medical services, and has also reduced the waiting time in the long lines for hospitals (particularly in the cities). A still greater reason to appreciate it is that it has allowed many "terminally ill" people to recover. In the area of sports, China has been quietly making use of chi gong as a method of raising the strength of its Olympic athletes, and they have won many gold, silver, and bronze medals.

In their practice of chi gong, the Chinese are seeking a state of "the unity of Heaven and man," a condition in which a person is at one with the universe. The moon, earth, sun, planets, and stars are filled with energy. When a person's body is completely relaxed and enters a meditative state, and is placed in a particular orientation, the human body will be in resonance with the fields of the universe, and the two will interact. When the person and the universe are in phase, the body's functioning will be better, and if they are out of phase, it will be worse. It is for this reason that constant practice of chi gong makes EHF more stable.

Chinese philosophy considers that all material in the universe consists of chi bodies. When the universe began, a kind of energy existed that the Chinese have called "chi." The nature of chi is dynamic. Its motions go through states of coalescing and joining, dissipating and dividing. All the things in the universe are produced through these movements and transformations of chi. The ancient Chinese doctors made use of this perspective in the development of medical science, and so they believed that chi was the basic element making up the human body. Further, they explained people's life development in terms of chi. If the internal chi is rich, the body will be strong and healthy. If not, it will suffer all sorts of ailments. In other words, if the internal chi is sufficient, a person's psychic abilities will be higher and will not suffer from falling power and instability.

Chinese medicine states that chi has many effects on the body. Some examples are:

A. *Immune effect:* In the last decade, Chinese scientists and Chinese and Western medical workers have proven that strong internal chi can raise the immune power of the body. Many people have overcome their diseases through the practice of chi gong, or have improved their conditions. A professor of immunology, Ms. Feng Lida of the Chinese Naval Hospital, has asserted that external chi was able to kill 60 percent of cancer cells in test tubes. Since ancient times, strengthening the internal chi has been a Chinese technique for promoting longevity. People who have practiced chi gong over a long period of time find that they catch colds seldom, if ever.

B. *Driving force:* The growth of the body, the circulation of the blood, the flow of the juices, all come from the stimulus and motive force of chi.

C. *Warming power:* The body maintains a normal temperature through the regulation of chi's warmth effect. Without this, the temperature loses control and becomes abnormal. The limbs will suffer the effects of coldness with this loss of the warming effect.

D. *The control effect on body fluids:* Chi controls the distribution of blood fluid, both stimulating its flow and keeping it under control. If a person's chi is weak, it can lead to bleeding or stagnant blood. In the same way, it also controls the sweat and urine, regulating their discharge. Weak chi can lead to night sweat, incontinence, or difficulty in urinating. Chi also has a filtering effect on the reproductive fluids. These fluids are depleted and thinned when a person's chi is weak. This can lead to impotence.

CHINA'S SUPER PSYCHICS

E. *Balancing the* yin *and* yang: This is a rather complicated matter. The Chinese yin-yang concept states that the universe is a material whole arising out of the opposition of the yin (negative) and yang (positive) energies. Anything in Heaven or on earth contains elements of this duality, such as male and female, motion and stillness, day and night, and so on. It is the movements and transformations of yin and yang that give rise to everything in the universe, and propels them to develop and change. Yin-yang expresses a concept of things that are opposing and yet interdependent. For this reason, yin and yang can evolve into each other, and all things can be analyzed into a yin and a yang component. These components themselves can be further subdivided into their own yin and yang subcomponents, and this breaking down into parts can be continued indefinitely. This phenomenon of things existing both in opposition and in combination can be seen everywhere in the natural world.

Neither yin nor yang can exist in isolation from the other. For example, if there were no left (yin) there could be no right (yang), if there were no up (yang) there could be no down (yin), if there were no heat (yang) there could be no cold (yin). Yang depends on yin, just as yin depends on yang. However, yin and yang are not frozen in a static position. They are in a state of flux that can be characterized as "yang receding and yin growing" or "yin receding and yang growing." For instance, in the four seasons of the year, there are changes from the warmth of spring to the heat of summer, the cool of autumn and the cold of winter. This process shows "yin receding and yang growing," followed by "yang receding and yin growing."

Paul Dong and Thomas Raffill

In terms of the human body, the production of all kinds of functions (yang) must expend some of the nutrients in the body (yin), and the metabolic processing of these nutrients must expend a certain amount of energy. These are processes of "yang receding and yin growing" and "yin receding and yang growing." In normal conditions, this "ebb and flow of yin and yang" exists in a fairly stable equilibrium, but if the receding and growing becomes unbalanced and goes beyond the normal bounds, the body will experience an oversupply of one aspect and an undersupply of the other. This leads to disease.

Thus, in order to maintain the balance of yin and yang, the body must have enough supply of strong chi (energy) to serve this need. To gain a supply of strong chi, in addition to good nutrition, sleep and exercise, it is also important to do chi gong exercises. Besides its own inherent advantages, chi gong can also compensate for insufficient nutrition (you may refer to the material on *bi gu* or meditative fasting elsewhere in the book), insufficient sleep, or insufficient exercise.

Many civilizations (especially ancient ones) have their own meditation systems, and these are all similar to chi gong in their basic principles. If you want to choose one of the better practices, it would be best to search for one from China's 3,000 years of tradition. Based on my own experience, I am happy to introduce a chi gong practice combining movement with stillness. China has many movement exercises, and everyone can choose his or her own favorite. Stillness refers to the lack of movement, such as meditation, silent sitting, standing, or lying down.

The method of practice is: First, do any movement exercise for half an hour, then meditate for an hour (start with a half hour the first time, and gradually practice longer every day up to an hour). This technique will give your body rich energy. The spirit is concentrated, the vital forces rich, and all body functions will be at their best.

Why do we have to practice chi gong to attain these benefits? As the saying goes, "Nothing in the world comes without working for it." Chi is the same way. If you don't practice, it won't come. It is a thing we usually can't see or perceive, it doesn't work at its full potential, and only appears in special conditions. What are these conditions, then? *Huang Di Nei Jing (The Yellow Emperor's Classic of Internal Medicine)*, a famous ancient Chinese medical encyclopedia, says, "Be imperturbable and the true chi will come to you, concentrate the inner spirit and well-being will follow." To explain this in modern terms, the mind should be quiet, empty, without desire, noncontrolling, light, harmonious. . . . Such are the conditions in which chi will appear and be of benefit to the health and the development of latent abilities.

When we treat a disease with acupuncture, if we want to have *de chi* (a technical term in acupuncture, referring to the sensation of chi flowing after an acupuncture point is needled), we must follow this principle. *The Yellow Emperor's Classic of Internal Medicine* points out the importance of "healing the spirit" (the spirit must be concentrated, and the attention should be focused on the patient) when doing needling. Thus, chi is related to the spirit, and chi only appears in particular spiritual states. These states are meditation, relaxation, and concentration. This is recorded in the ancient texts, and modern practitioners have confirmed it. When judging the skill of an acupuncturist, you should also apply this principle in making your choice. If the doctor is absentminded and not focused on the patient during treatment, you would be wise to avoid him or her.

Although chi gong can produce EHF and raise the functioning of the body, not everybody can be good at it. Generally speaking, out of every thousand people sensitive to chi, one to three will attain EHF. Those not sensitive to chi will produce no effects. As of now, the world does not have any kind of measuring instrument to tell us whether a person is sensitive to chi. The only way we can tell who is sensitive is to have a chi gong master send external chi to a person. I often send external chi to my students or to people seeking a healing to test their sensitivity, and I have strong experience in this regard.

Why is it that only those sensitive to chi can develop EHF? The reason is that chi can activate the hidden potentials of the body. If you are sensitive to chi, you will naturally feel the effects, but if you are not, you won't feel anything. This is the same as people who are more susceptible to liquor or people with sensitive skin. When we practice chi gong and enter a relaxed, meditative state, the rate of blood flow increases, the temperature rises, the breathing slows, the internal body feels as though a light electric current is flowing through it; it feels like stepping into a magnetic field, the body becomes light and seems to float, the mood is cheerful, and it feels like another world. Clearly, these things create good conditions for activating the latent potentials of the body.

I believe that in the not-too-distant future, scientists or psychic researchers will tell us more about how chi gong opens the special abilities, so that we can learn more and make the best use of this natural treasure to benefit humankind.

• 9 •

The Psychic Children of China and Their Training

C hina is sometimes said to be the fourth-most-powerful nation in the world. Its current population is 1.2 billion, but in 1979, the year EHF was discovered, it was a "mere" one billion (the 0.2 billion increase since then is close to the population of the entire U.S.). Based on the approximation that one out of a million people has EHF, China would have 1,000 people with EHF in a population of one billion. The great majority of these are children. This is because after people with EHF pass the age of twenty-five, their powers tend to gradually weaken and disappear.

You may not have known that China has so many children with EHF. In addition to those born with the powers, there are many others who came from a national training program implemented in China's elementary schools since 1981. The researchers used all kinds of techniques to bring out their powers, including hypnotic suggestion, psychological influence, chi energy fields and chi transmission, external chi from chi gong masters, stimulation of the acupuncture points, speech, and pictures. Within a year, the number of children whose powers were brought out by these techniques had reached three thousand. Zhang Yansheng, one of China's super psychics known as "China's modern-day wizard," has personally assisted in the EHF training of as many as 500 children.

Why would the Chinese government be interested in providing EHF training to children? Researchers believe that everyone has untapped powers, and the only difference from one person to another is in the number and degree of these powers. If a person has rich untapped powers, these will manifest themselves when the right time comes in the person's life. However, if these are stimulated by training techniques, the EHF can appear sooner, although they may not appear in the case of people with weaker powers. Moreover, in most cases children's EHF powers appear from ages six to thirteen.

Induction of EHF in children in China began with some assistant professors in Beijing University who staked their careers on this research. They started in an elementary school, doing EHF induction and training with boys and girls around ten years old. To everyone's great surprise, 60 percent of them had powers like "reading with the ear." Feeling very excited about this, they published these results in *Nature Magazine*, and there was a huge response to this. After this, under the direction of scientists, tests were done on all elementary-school students in the country. The success rate was in the 30- to 40-percent range. The most exciting result came from Shanghai. The scientists achieved the highest success rates there in the six districts of Zhabei, Hongkou, Nanshi, Jiading, Changning, and Xuhui. The average for the whole city was

Fig. 9–1
In 1983, many of the elementary schools tested for psychic abilities. This is a picture after the test in one of the schools.

60 percent, including 30 percent of the children who developed the abilities after only one session, while the remaining 70 percent would require many sessions to bring out their powers. What is the reason that this second-largest city in the world achieved such a high score in child EHF development? Some joked that "all through its history, Shanghai has been a land of unknown supermen." It is true that Shanghai has many unusual things and unusual people, and is a city of mystery.

The high rate of success bringing out EHF in children in Shanghai might not be representative of other regions. Perhaps Shanghai is an isolated exception. In the Xuchang District of the city of Chongqing, testing was done on children age seven to twelve, and only thirteen out of sixty-nine were found to have EHF, for a rate of a mere 18.8 percent. This might be the district with the lowest rate. In general, looking at the figures for the whole country, the methods they used to bring out EHF were somewhere around 30 percent effective, in the sense that out of every hundred children, thirty would display EHF.

In light of this success in bringing out the powers in children, we might conclude that EHF is a natural gift, one possessed in greater or lesser degrees by all of us. This event also shows that EHF research should start with children. Although China has done a great deal of work in developing EHF in children, it has kept the research confidential. There are several reasons for this:

1. Children are the future wealth of the nation, and the nation has an obligation to protect them.
2. Most parents think that natural-born psychic powers are greater than those developed through training. They would not be happy for their children to be second-best and become "second-rate goods."
3. The EHF developed in the children was not stabilized, and so they might not want it to affect their mood.

Of course, they had other reasons as well. Thus, with few exceptions, among the EHF children discovered in China, we have no way of knowing which were natural-born and which were developed through training. The one thing we do know is that the number of children who developed EHF through training is many times higher than the natural-born number.

Although many people believe that natural-born psychic abilities are stronger than those derived through training, this is a misconception. Zhang Baosheng's abilities are inborn, while those of Yan Xin were produced through chi gong practice, and yet nobody has ever claimed that Zhang Baosheng's powers are stronger than Yan Xin's or the other way around. They are of equal rank in people's minds. Psychic powers should not be divided into the inborn and the trained, but rather into the many different kinds of abilities. For example, Yan Xin's EHF is generally strongest in healing, while Zhang Baosheng is not very good at healing. For this reason, few people ask Zhang Baosheng for healings. On the other hand, Zhang Baosheng can walk through walls and move objects with his mind, abilities that Yan Xin has never had. Psychic abilities are just like any other kind of abilities. Some people are very strong in math, but they may often be at the bottom of the class in writing and art. Some people like geography, some like astronomy. Everyone has his or her own strengths. Now let us introduce some of China's EHF children (some of these have grown up by now).

The first child we would like to introduce is Shen Kegong. At the age of thirteen, he calculated in his head the 26-digit solution to a math problem in twenty seconds. Because of this ability, he is known as "the supercomputer." Afraid that he may have made a mistake in the computation, or that there may have been a printing error in the published account, I spent two days to calculate 625^9 as: 14,551,915,228,366,851,806,640,625. Because I could not find an electric calculator or an abacus able to handle such a huge number, the only way I could do this task was to grind away at it with pen and paper for two days. I was deeply impressed, and I will never forget this wonder child of China, Shen Kegong.

Shen Kegong was discovered just twelve months after Tang Yu. According to his father, he and his mother had never noticed his amazing powers of calculation before. His

Fig. 9–2
China's "supercomputer," Shen Kegong, a thirteen-year-old prodigy who takes twenty
seconds to give an answer to $625^9 = 14,551,915,228,366,851,806,640,625$.

father recalled one time when he, Kegong's mother, and Kegong were going out shopping. Just as his mother was about to pay, he told her she had made a miscalculation. When she worked it out a second time, she found she had indeed made a mistake. Shen Kegong's father is himself a master on the abacus and works as an accountant for a production line. His son would often play beside him. Whenever he made a mistake, his son would point it out. At first he thought his son was trying to make mischief, but he later discovered that he really had made a mistake. After many similar experiences, he learned that his son was a wonder child.

1980 was Shen Kegong's lucky year. On September 18 of that year, Shanxi Province held a province-wide abacus contest, and 1,200 people took part, among them Shen Kegong.

CHINA'S SUPER PSYCHICS

The categories covered in the contest included multidigit integers, decimals, fractional arithmetic, squares, and square roots, among others. The result of the contest was that he calculated the solution to $639 \times 33 + \sqrt[3]{884,736} = 21,183$ faster than either an abacus or an electric calculator (it took him 3.4 seconds). Later that year, the Central Finance and Economics College and the China Abacus Association jointly sponsored a Shen Kegong Rapid Calculation Exposition. Hundreds of people took part in the competition, and they tried as many as twenty categories of operations. Once again, Shen Kegong was able to get all the answers rapidly. Some examples are $4,789,240 \div 45 = 106,427.555$ (1.6 seconds); $35 \times 45 \times 25 = 39,375$ (1.8 seconds) . . . and so on. Of course, his most brilliant performance was in the China Agricultural Bank, where, watched by all the employees of the bank, he calculated 625^9 in twenty seconds. The observers all broke out in cheers and applause. Since then, he has been China's number one supercomputer.

In Shanghai there is a girl named Xiao Xiong whose EHF was discovered when she was eleven years old. Xiao Xiong's father is said to be very interested in EHF research. One day, he said to his daughter, "How about having a reading test?" She nodded in agreement, and so he placed in her pencil case a piece of paper on which he had written the Chinese characters *yellow dog* and asked her to try to read it. Xiao Xiong concentrated her mind and stared at the pencil case. After about ten seconds, she said that she saw the words *yellow dog* written in red on the paper. Her father was delighted, and opened the case to take out the paper. At this moment, he discovered that another copy of the words *yellow dog* were written in pencil on top of the folded paper. He was very puzzled. Looking closely, he recognized the pencil writing as his daughter's handwriting. This surprised him all the more.

He wrote the characters *yellow dog* in red pen himself. He had not written anything else in pencil. He quickly asked his daughter how this had happened. She said she didn't know how the additional words appeared on the paper, but she remembered going over the writing of these characters in her head while reading them. Her father paid great attention when he heard this. After this, her father asked her to try another reading test. This time, he wrote the characters for *high mountain flowing water* in blue ink. He also told her to go over the writing of them in her head when she read them. The result was that she recognized the words *high mountain flowing water* in under two minutes, and then went over their writing in her head. When her father opened the case, sure enough, the paper had another copy of the words in pencil.

Her father was excited to learn that his daughter had this kind of power. The next day, he asked her to try a test writing on a blank piece of paper. He took a sheet on which nothing at all was written, and put it into the pencil case along with a pencil. He asked her to imagine writing whatever words she thought of. She agreed and sat in a chair, thinking quietly. In a while, she said she had finished writing the characters for *hello* in her mind. Her father immediately opened the case to take a look, and indeed, the characters for *hello* were written in pencil on the sheet. Then he asked his daughter to try it again several times, and she succeeded every time. She produced sometimes one word, sometimes two, or five or six, whatever happened to come into her head.

Xiao Xiong's father reported this new discovery to local EHF researchers. They also tested Xiao Xiong's ability repeatedly and confirmed it. Afterward, they termed this type of EHF "psychic writing."

Xiao Xiong, with her abilities described above, is by no means the only child in China with the "psychic writing" ability. In 1981, EHF researchers at Yunnan Wenshan Teachers' College in Yunnan Province selected five children with EHF for further training. At the start, the only thing these children could do was to read with the ear. But after a week, they had developed to a point where they could read with their fingers, palms, toes, and the soles of their feet, as well as the "third eye" point on the forehead. Their powers were getting stronger every day, and after a month of this training, they could reset the hands of a watch by mind power.

Later, due to personnel changes, the research project on training the five EHF children was turned over to Department Two of the Yunnan Province Geological Survey. They began by selecting the child identified as H (none of the subjects of the tests were willing to release their names) to test the ability to do "psychic writing." Five people supervised the experiments. The chief researcher, Zhao Yun, placed a blank sheet of paper and a blue inkpen in a folder. The cap of the pen was left on, however. The folder was sealed tight with adhesive tape. Child H was instructed to think of the Chinese characters for *precious object*. He placed the folder under the left foot, and then looked up and gazed forward. After one minute, H said, "It is finished," and Zhao Yun opened the folder. The words "precious object" were written on the paper in blue ink.

After this, the chief researcher Zhao Yun asked to do another test. This time, he used a pen that had a switch for changing colors, putting it in a folder with a blank sheet and sealing it with tape. This time H was asked to write the words *precious object* in red ink. H agreed to do this and began writing mentally. This time, the child took two minutes before saying it was done. In the presence of the group of observers, Zhao Yun opened the folder, and the words *precious object* were written in red ink as desired.

Later, eight people at a school called Wenshan First Middle School, including Principal Zhao Bixin and Vice Principal Li Chenghua, conducted similar experiments in all aspects of psychic writing with children identified as C, G, Z, and Y. All of these were successful. Altogether they conducted fifty-nine experiments over the period from October 4, 1981, to November 20, 1983. (Note that the children's names were only given in first initials at the request of the children and their parents.)

Of all the psychic phenomena, I have always most admired telepathy and opening flowers. A Chinese saying goes, "*A flower opens to prosperity.*" When Chinese New Year comes, everyone posts papers with greetings like "*Happy New Year*" and "*A flower opens to prosperity,*" symbolizing the good fortune of the coming spring. The opening of a flower is thought to bring good fortune. There are a number of EHF phenomena involving flower opening, and these have been reported in newspapers and magazines under many curious headlines, such as "Why Do the Flowers Bloom Early," "Flowers Flying Everywhere in the Spring City," "Why the Flowers are So Beautiful," and "Flowers Blooming Like Crazy." Let us look at a few of these reports now.

The climate in the city of Kunming, in Yunnan Province in southern China, is springlike all year round. For this reason, it is known as "Spring City." Since spring is the time when flowers bloom, and the Kunming City government has paid much attention to planting flowers, the city is covered with flowers blooming in the springtime. One of the "psychic flower blooming" incidents was well described by the newspaper headline, "Flowers Flying Everywhere in the Spring City."

Zhu Yiyi, editor of Shanghai's *Nature Magazine*, is a leading pioneer in researching children's EHF and developing (or training) their powers. One day, she came to Kunming to meet with Yunnan University's Professor Luo, Professor Zheng, and Xiao Li, Xiao Yan, Xiao Ling, and Xiao Chun for experiments in opening flowers. Each of these girls was given a china vase covered with its top. The supervisors of the experiment told them to pick flowers with their mind power, any flowers or flower buds they liked. At this time, the supervisors kept a close watch over the vases in the girls' hands.

When the four children tried to pick flowers with their mind power, the first to shout out was Xiao Li. With an excited expression, she shouted that she'd got it. She was so happy because this was the first time she'd ever succeeded in picking flowers with her mind. She had picked a winter jasmine bud. When the other three girls heard that Xiao Li had done it, it added to their own confidence, and so it was not long until they all started shouting, "The flower has come," one after another. When the tops were opened, one had a leaf of a tree, one had a flower bud, and one had a beautiful flower in full bloom.

The test of the four children lasted thirty minutes altogether, and they gathered a total of thirty-five winter jasmines, buds, and tree leaves. But in Xiao Li's vase, they discovered a bud of a tea plant. One of the test monitors, Mr. Yang, was very surprised and thought there was something special about this flower bud. He went home to his balcony, and his rare breed of tea, that he had been cultivating for three years until it finally put out a flower bud this year, was gone, picked by the psychic girl. However, while chagrined about his loss, he was excited about the success of picking flowers by mind power. The experience brought him a mixture of happiness and sadness.

These tests of gathering or opening flowers led by Ms. Zhu Yiyi, raised the question of "why the flowers open early."

One time, when she was describing psychic flower opening, Ms. Zhu pointed out that modern biological science tells us that living things are governed by natural laws. The blooming of a flower is closely related to its biological stages. This being so, why is EHF able to violate these biological laws and make a flower bud open early? This is a matter that we will need the help of biologists to study.

At the end of 1980, six psychic children, including Xiao Pan, Xiao Zhang, and Xiao Li, were invited to demonstrate flower opening. Before the demonstration, many azalea buds were picked and distributed to the six children, the buds placed in plastic containers. Seven minutes after the start, Xiao Pan said the flowers were fully opened. Ten minutes later, Xiao Zhang said her flowers were only half opened. The other four children all said their flowers were fully opened. The monitors checked each of these, and they found that Xiao Zhang's flowers were only half opened, the others were fully opened.

EHF children can make a hundred flowers bloom, but what is the process by which they open? To answer this question, they asked Xiao Pan to give a demonstration of flower opening by herself. They gave her a carnation bud, which was tightly closed. Then, Xiao Pan held the stem of the carnation tight, and she stared intently at the flower bud. The observers all around were watching her with bated breath. After about ten minutes, the flower bloomed before the eyes of all the observers. It was like seeing a slow-motion film. Everyone praised the accomplishment. This was a rare, once-in-a-lifetime spectacle.

During 1993 and 1994, Beijing author Ke Yunlu organized a film crew to make a documentary called *An Investigation of Life's Extraordinary Phenomena*. They filmed EHF presentations all over China. The whole documentary was in twenty-four forty-five-minute parts, all on different themes. Thirteen videos have come out, one of which is on the theme "Developing the Latent Powers of Children." This video is about a project in which chi gong master Liang Guangxiang selected eleven students (four boys and seven girls) from Dong Si Shi Tiao Elementary School in Beijing for EHF training. The time was the morning of January 16, 1994, and the place was Beijing's Guanyuan Children's Activity Center. Master Liang had the schoolchildren relax, close their eyes, and sit silently. Then he sent external chi to them and told them to visualize the night sky and imagine a ball of light getting brighter and brighter. After about ten minutes, he told them to imagine this ball of light shining brilliantly inside their own bodies. Then he told them to look inside themselves. Soon afterward, some of them said they could see their own blood vessels, bones, heart, stomach, and so on. (Caution to readers: Do not attempt this without the supervision of a doctor or chi gong master.)

Liang Guangxiang has done this kind of training and activation of children's latent powers on various occasions and in various circumstances over ten different times. From teaching children to see inside themselves, he has gone on to teach them to see the internal organs of other people and to see through objects. His training starts out on a light level, and then gets deeper and deeper, gradually strengthening the children's powers. He has a success rate of 80 percent, and with one group of children the powers reached 100 percent. They were tested in the presence of monitors to assure the credibility of the results. These monitors included Assistant Professor Xu Yan (female) of the Psychology Department of Beijing Teachers' College, a (male) reporter from *Guangming Ribao*, head doctor Cheng Xiaofen (female) of the Optometry Department of Beijing Medical School, and others.

Beijing has a pair of sisters, Wang Qiang, the elder sister, age thirteen when discovered, and Wang Bin, the younger, age eleven when discovered (*see chapter 3*). Initially their powers were reading and color perception by ear, fingers, and armpit, and telepathy. The latter power was particularly strong. For this reason, many researchers used them as the subjects in telepathy experiments. It is reported that over fifty tests of their telepathy powers have been done.

These included one administered by the film crew of *An Investigation of Life's Extraordinary Phenomena*. On February 20 in the Beijing Modern Information Development Center, they conducted a demonstration of the telepathy of the two sisters Wang Qiang and Wang Bin. They performed a matching task with toy blocks, using telepathy. The two sisters had often played this game when they were little girls. One of them would make one figure with blocks, and the other, located in another place, would use telepathy to make the same figure. On this day, the procedure was to be certified by several observers placed at various locations. These observers were not permitted to move or talk. Wang Qiang and Wang Bin were each given similar sets of blocks. Wang Bin sat quietly, but after Wang Qiang had arranged some blocks, Wang Bin got to work on the task. Following Wang Qiang's thoughts, she arranged her blocks piece by piece. In the end, the two block figures made by the girls came out the same.

In fact, telepathic block-arranging is a new and interesting game. I know of an even more interesting event at a demonstration by Wang Qiang and Wang Bin. On November 19, 1993, in a demonstration of reading with the fingers at Sitong Company in Beijing, President Ni Zhiwei of Beijing's Haihua Company wrote the five English letters *H H N Z W* in a sealed and opaque envelope, handing it to Wang Bin to read with her fingers. After taking the envelope and feeling over it, she perceived the five English letters *H H Z Z V*. Here is the problem. You may say she was wrong, but you could also

Fig. 9–3
Famous writer Xiao Jun and his wife examining the EHF of Wang Qiang (left) and Wang Bin. The photo was taken after the examination. (photo courtesy of Zhou Wen Bin).

say she was partly right. *H H* was correct, the third letter *Z* was an *N* turned sideways, and the letter *V* is part of an *W*.

In fact, many young children can perform similar feats. I observed this personally on a trip to Shanghai where I attended a public EHF performance. Two young girls on stage were doing reading with their ears and armpits. An assistant went through the audience asking people to write something down on a piece of paper, and these were folded and placed in a box to test the girls' abilities. I volunteered to write something twice, and the first time they got it right. The second time, I wrote two letters of the Russian alphabet, **Я Н**. One girl wrote on the blackboard what she saw, **Я Н**, which was correct. The second girl wrote the **Я** backward, as though it were an *R*. It seems to be a common mistake for the images visualized to be turned around in some way like this. After the show, I also managed to talk to the girls a little. They told me they first learned of their powers when a school-wide testing program discovered their sensitivity and they were selected for training. They also described to me the process of seeing in their minds, saying they would feel a numbness and buzzing sensation and then they would get visions that could be brought into focus.

As I learned upon further investigation, the reason for the fame of Wang Qiang and Wang Bin is that they developed many more powers beyond those simple ones they had at first. These include restoring a torn card, removing pills from a medicine bottle by mind power, psychic writing, restoring broken chinaware, mineral prospecting, and healing. Anyone who does EHF research should know that EHF can be strengthened. It can also be weakened through either overuse or disuse. This conforms to a "use it or lose it" principle in evolution, whereby faculties that are being used tend to become stronger. In addition, even a person who has no EHF abilities at all can be trained.

Professor Song Kongzhi, who has researched EHF for years, says there is nothing mystical about EHF phenomena. Using scientifically based training techniques, it is quite possible to turn a person with no EHF to one who does have EHF.

In the past decade, China has systematically compiled the experiences of psychic children all over the country, combined these with psychological theory, and used the information as the basis for creating a method for training psychic children. In addition, they have designed a method of training groups of young adults age fifteen to twenty. Each group would undergo ten days of training, with training every day early in the morning and in the afternoon (after a noon nap),

Fig. 9–4
Zhu Yiyi (center), editor for *Nature Magazine*, who is a specialist in organizing research on EHF Children; at right is Paul Dong, and at left is a Shanghai chi gong master.

one hour for each training session. The first item they worked on was "non-eye-based vision," because this is an ability that is relatively easy to produce. After succeeding at this, they moved on to more advanced skills. During the training for "non-eye-based vision," the success rate for groups of children has been around 30 to 40 percent, while in groups of teenagers it is only 3 percent, an order of magnitude lower.

When researchers were first starting to train children nationwide, proponents and opponents were still in the midst of the debate on the existence of psychic phenomena. This made it impossible to implement training programs on as large a scale as they would have liked. They also met with many obstacles in carrying out their plans. However, their experiments in training finally did show that EHF can be induced.

Professor Song Kongzhi has said that the main reasons that young children have a higher success rate than teenagers or above is that they have less cluttered minds, making them better at concentrating and more receptive to psychological direction, while the contrary is true for teenagers. During the training process, both groups of children and groups of teenagers experience physiological reactions, such as throbbing heads and sensations of anxiety, but these symptoms are more pronounced among the teenagers. This is probably because young children have stronger adaptability to these stresses.

One of the notable features of their child EHF development training is that girls are easier to train than boys. Any child who develops EHF in three days must be a girl. From this it could be surmised that China's top super psychic must be a lady. More will be revealed about this in chapter 11.

· 10 ·

How to Create the Third Eye

W hen asked what the third eye is, Westerners and Easterners may have different responses. The first thing thought of by most Chinese would be the god Erlang from the famous, centuries-old, classic novel *Xi You Ji* (*Journey to the West*, also translated as *Monkey*). Between his two eyes, Erlang had grown an extra one that could see for a thousand miles and had terrifying powers. *Journey to the West* is one of the most widely published and distributed books in Chinese history. A quest fantasy based on Buddhism, it is a marvelous work attractive to children and adults alike. Every year, this book sells millions of copies, and you wouldn't be able to find anyone in China who had never heard of the god Erlang and his deadly foe, Monkey King. Monkey King's "golden fire eye" was just as powerful as god Erlang's third eye, and could both see through objects and tell truth from falsehood. These third eyes of Monkey King and the god Erlang are examples of the Buddha eye of the Buddhist masters. This is one of their highest spiritual powers.

The Chinese teachings of Taoism and Buddhism both have third eyes, and the differences between the two are minor. People usually associate the third eye more with Buddhism. The Buddhists speak of the *wu yan tong*—"five spiritual penetrations" or "five eyes of mastery"—which consist of the *rou yan tong* or "flesh eye"; *tian yan tong* or "heavenly eye" (this is what we call the third eye); *hui yan tong* or "wisdom eye"; *fa yan tong* or "dharma eye"; and *fo yan tong* or "Buddha eye." Each of these represents a different stage of development, going higher and higher. Now, let us first come to understand what these five eyes are, and then discuss the third eye.

The flesh eye refers to an eye superior to ordinary people's. Others cannot see clearly objects that are at a distance, or very small, or dimly lit, but your eyes can see anything, no matter how far, how small, or how dark. As you practice this skill, your sharpness of vision is raised, and this leads you to the attainment of the flesh eye. Further practice will with time lead you to progress to the next stage, the heavenly eye.

The heavenly eye (third eye) is not an ordinary eye, but the *tian mu* acupuncture point (also called *bai hui* acupuncture point). When it is opened, it brings the powers of remote viewing or see-through vision. Remote viewing is also called the thousand-mile eye. But unlike the distance vision of the flesh eye, it uses the mind instead of the eye to see things. See-through vision was called ghost vision by the ancients. Actually, it is not ghosts, but one of the special powers of the body.

Most people would think that having attained the heavenly eye, they are at the top and their power is great. Actually, the heavenly eye is only one stage beyond the flesh eye, and is nowhere near the highest levels of attainment. The heavenly eye can only visualize things in the mind, but cannot reveal more of their details. For example, it might see the front of the object but not be able to see the back, or only see the top without seeing the bottom. It cannot feel the texture of the object, know if it is made of wood or of ceramic, what color it is, what it was like ten years earlier. . . . But if you attain the wisdom eye, you will not only see the whole object, you will also be able to tell its past and future. For example, you might be able to tell that a ceramic object had been through a fire ten years ago and was slightly damaged, was recently filled with vinegar, and so on, in great detail. The wisdom eye is quite a high-level skill. The Chinese have a saying, *"to get to know people through the wisdom eye,"* meaning to have the ability to choose good people for one's friends.

Of course, the dharma eye is an even higher stage than the wisdom eye. The dharma eye not only has all the powers of the wisdom eye, it also has very high energy and lights the universe. It also has the power to repair things. For example, in the case mentioned above of the ceramic object damaged by fire, if you have the dharma eye you can repair the broken part and make it as good as new. A master of the dharma-eye skill can snap a steel wire with his gaze, and can also repair a broken piece.

It would seem that extremely few people can attain the Buddha eye. In the annals of Buddhist history, only the Lord Buddha and his disciples were said to have this power. As the Buddhists say, "Buddhism is boundless," meaning there is nothing it cannot do. The Buddha eye can see the past and the future, light the universe, change the course of events, and change matter in the universe. Its power covers the universe, and when it reaches the stage of "Buddha light shining every-where," anything in the range lit by the Buddha light will be controlled and changed by it, including people's fate.

The wisdom eye, dharma eye, and Buddha eye are deep and abstruse mysteries of Buddhism, and are beyond our ability to explain in this brief introduction, so it would be better for us to turn our attention to the heavenly eye and see what it is like. Although the heavenly eye has some special powers different from the flesh eye, it still includes the usual flesh-eye abilities. The heavenly eye is unstable and can be lost. Because of this, we can conclude that in the transition between them, the difference is not qualitative, but quantita-tive. Most quantitative differences can be turned back easily, but qualitative differences are difficult to reverse. This is why the heavenly eye is still a skill on a low level of EHF. If one attains the wisdom eye, this is a qualitatively different skill, and a high level of EHF.

Since the heavenly eye is a low-level EHF, it is not so dif-ficult to attain, particularly for children and young adults. At an age before their powers start to weaken, they can develop it through chi gong practice. For children, it may not even be necessary to practice chi gong, and they can be trained by psychological methods of induction. Certain adults with the right characteristics can still attain it even after the age when their powers have weakened, by practicing chi gong.

The idea behind practicing the heavenly eye is very simple. As Lu Mianchuan, a human body science researcher from China's Sichuan Province, has said, Buddhists view the eyes, ears, nose, tongue, body, and mind (*yi* or intention) as the six stems (or the six uses). The six stems all belong to *yi* (inten-tion), because intention is the source of the other five uses. For example, when the mind is connected with the eyes, we see images, and when it is connected with the ears, we hear sounds. However, if the links with the mind are cut off, they are empty shells, and the same is true for the nose, tongue, and body. The eyes and ears are tools for sight and hearing, but on the more fundamental level, thought is the source of sight and hearing. If the tools (five stems) can be used, they can also be changed. This is why thought can change the uses of the five stems (such as using the ear in place of the eye).

Moreover, the six stems contain opposites of yin and yang, tangible and intangible. To be specific, the eye sees visible objects (that are tangible, and so, yang), and the ear hears invisible sounds (intangible, or yin). The scents smelled by the nose are intangible (yin), things tasted are tangible (yang), and the body's sense of touch is tangible (yang), while the mind's thoughts are intangible (yin). Yin, yang, intangible, and tangible are opposites, and so they can be transformed (*refer to the explanation of the yin-yang concept in chapter 8*). Thus, Buddhism claims that the six stems are a false distinction and they are actually interchangeable. The only reason they are not mixed is the fixations in people's minds. Today this philosophy has been partially confirmed, for example, in the current cases all over China of EHF children reading with their ears, underarms, fingers, and so on. All these are evidence of the interchangeability of the six stems. And the use of the heavenly eye (third eye) to see things by thought power is based on the same principles.

Many people have had the following experience: When sitting in meditation with the eyes closed, with the mind not thinking of any other things, he or she will have some kind of sensitivity. If a person softly comes into the area or from behind, he or she will immediately sense the presence of the person. Young people are much more sensitive in this way than older people, and little children are the most sensitive of all. This is EHF, but one of a low level. To raise its level and increase its sensitivity, one can practice chi gong exercises or Western psychic training.

The following is my own third eye training regimen:

1. Sit down on a comfortable chair, halfway in the seat, with the hands placed on the knees. Close the eyes and relax the whole body.
2. Lightly rub the third eye position on the forehead three times.
3. Block out distracting thoughts and sit silently for about ten minutes. Then, visualize the third eye breathing (but only concentrating on inhaling, not exhaling) three times. Actually the nose is breathing these three times, and you simply imagine that the air is entering through the third eye. After three times, resume breathing normally.
4. After waiting another ten minutes, begin circulating your chi (energy) from the *dan tian* (located about two inches below the navel) downward, over the *hui yin, ming men, da zhu, yu zhen, bai hui* (top of the head), and then down the *yin tang* (third eye position), *ren zhong, cheng liang, tian tu, shan zhong,* and back again to the *dan tian*. These are the names of eleven acupuncture points on the body. If you don't want to learn and memorize these, you can simply learn that you move your chi from the *dan tian* downward, over the genital area, up the back, straight to the tip of the head, then down to the third eye position (between the two eyebrows), and then down to the *dan tian* point in a straight line. With the chi energy slowly circulating like this, practice for five minutes. The Chinese call this *xiao zhou tian* ("the small circuit"). The small circuit is a health-promoting practice, but also an EHF practice that can open the heavenly eye.
5. When the chi has returned to the *dan tian* point, concentrate

on the *dan tian* for five minutes. Then, slowly open the eyes, stand up, and begin the ending exercise.

As a rule in the practice of Chinese chi gong, all practice must conclude with an ending exercise. Otherwise, the body may experience some discomfort. By doing the ending exercise, you return to the normal state. The following are the steps for the ending exercise:

1. After opening the eyes and standing, raise your arms in front of your chest, bring the palms together, and rub them until they get warm. Rub the hands over the face as if washing your face. Do this ten times (rubbing from the front of the face to the neck counts as one time).
2. With the arms in front of the chest, move your chi down toward the *dan tian*. Repeat this several times.
3. Repeatedly pat down your left arm with your right hand from top to bottom.
4. Repeatedly pat down your right arm with your left hand from top to bottom.
5. Repeatedly pat down the legs with both hands, from top to bottom.

Practice this every morning after waking up and every evening before bed for one hour.

These procedures are used for the first three months of practice. After three months, the procedure changes as follows:

1. Sit halfway on a chair, with the hands placed on the knees. Close your eyes and relax your whole body.
2. Empty your mind. Imagine that the heavenly eye has opened. A light goes from the *bai hui* point on the top of

your head into your body, lighting up your head and then spreading down and lighting up your whole body.

3. Sit silently in meditation for ten minutes. Imagine the third eye breathing, then return to normal and do the "small circuit" chi circulation through the front and back of the body, and continue gradually circulating for ten minutes (it was only five minutes in the first three months). Finally, move the chi back to the *dan tian*.

4. After the chi returns to the *dan tian*, concentrate on the *dan tian* for ten minutes before doing the ending exercise.

Do this once or twice every day. Note that is most important to do it at least once in the morning.

Do this second set of exercises for three months. Then, you can move on to the third set of exercises as follows:

1. Sit silently, close the eyes, relax, empty your mind. Imagine that the third eye opens slightly. At first you see a light in the darkness, like the glow of a TV screen, and then an object appears steadily in this glow. While doing this visualization, do not try to force things. If you see something, that's great, but if you don't, you don't.

2. If you don't see anything in this light the first time, you may attempt to see a familiar object placed on the table (only one item, and not for very long). For example, you may place a watch on the table. Try to do this, but do not force yourself.

3. If you cannot see the watch, you may visualize your internal organs, for example, your intestines, stomach, lungs, liver, kidney, and so on, or you may visualize your blood flowing.

4. If you don't see the above, you may begin by visualizing the face and the smile of your spouse (or a person you

want to see). If this succeeds, you can move on to the next step and try to visualize the other items mentioned above.

With the above training, you should see things within about a month. If you do not accomplish it in a month, you may give up, because not everyone is able to develop the third-eye skill. It is easily attained only by the young and by those sensitive to chi, and particularly the latter. For example, acupuncture and energy healing are more effective on some, less effective on others, and is ineffective on still others. This depends on the sensitivity of the person. For example, for a person highly sensitive to chi, this technique might be 98 percent effective, for one only half sensitive, it might be 40 percent effective, and so on.

If we know whether we are sensitive to chi, we can save a great deal on medical expenses (for example, by acupuncture and energy healing), and can avoid the need for critical measures in emergencies. If we don't know our level of sensitivity, there are two methods for finding out. Of course, the best method of testing it is to have a chi gong master send chi to your palm. A second way is to try a thermographic test. Western countries have developed a kind of thermographic scanner that can show the sensitivity and strength of chi, but it is rather expensive. I have often helped people determine their sensitivity to chi, and people have always expressed their satisfaction.

· 11 ·

The Modern Goddess of Mercy

C hina has twenty-nine provinces and 1.2 billion people, for an average of about 40 million people in each province—about 20 million more than California, the most populous state in the U.S. The higher the population a place has, the more extraordinary people it will have in its midst. Every province is full of unknown but amazing people. Moreover, for reasons discussed earlier, the most economically deprived province must be the one with the most super psychics. This is one of the reasons it is doubtful that the U.S. could have large numbers of super psychics. If you pay a little attention, you will notice that two or three out of every four people, particularly men, are overweight, with large bellies. This is a sign of a rich diet. As the people live in an environment with an abundant supply of food available with little effort, they become fat and damage their health, but another consequence of this is that they will not become super psy-

CHINA'S SUPER PSYCHICS

chics. The highest-level people of special abilities usually come from poor or developing nations, such as was the case in China and India in the past. Since the 1990s, China has been experiencing an economic takeoff, and the people in the coastal regions are becoming more prosperous. The proportion of super psychics should decrease along with this trend. The super psychics described below were born in the 1970s and 1980s, and each one is more powerful than the last. This also includes China's top super psychic.

A Lady of Many Abilities—Yao Zheng

I would like to first discuss Yao Zheng, a pretty and innocent young lady. In October 1991, I accepted an invitation to Yao Zheng's home in the Tanggu District of Tianjin City, accompanied by three editors for *The Journal of UFO Research*, a publication of the Gansu Province Publishing House. She would demonstrate her multifaceted EHF abilities. I am a friend of her father's and had come a long way from America, and they showed great hospitality and asked me to stay in their home. Yao Zheng herself moved into the guest room to let me use her room. I was afraid it would disturb her sleep and affect her EHF abilities, but as events showed, this fear was unnecessary.

The four of us (the other was the driver, who was also a member of the Chinese UFO Research Society), arrived at her home at eleven o'clock in the morning. After having lunch, we couldn't wait to see Yao Zheng demonstrate her EHF.

I had brought my own spoon, of a particularly solid consistency, to use during the demonstration. In addition, in a hotel pharmacy, I had bought a bottle of white medicine pills for inflammations (some medicines that are impossible to buy

Fig. 11–1
Yao Zheng is using mind power to make vitamin pills come out of a bottle.

in the U.S. can be easily bought over-the-counter in Hong Kong and China). I was planning to have Yao Zheng use these to demonstrate her ability to "move pills through bottles." To my surprise, her father, Mr. Yao Wenji, was against using these pills. The reason was that the pills were for inflammations, and he was afraid they would go into Yao Zheng's stomach. He explained that there had been many cases in China when, in EHF demonstrations of "moving pills through bottles," some pills ended up in the stomach of the person giving the demonstration.

For safety's sake, he suggested that I purchase some harmless product such as vitamin pills. This made sense, and I went out and bought a new bottle of Chinese vitamin pills for the demonstration. The pills were black, the kind they make in China.

After I returned from the shop, the first demonstration was "moving pills through bottles." Besides being corked shut, Chinese medicine bottles are sealed with wax, which will break whenever anyone opens the bottle. On top of that, there is a twist-off cover to protect the neck of the bottle. After Yao Zheng took the bottle, she concentrated her mind on it, sometimes shaking it lightly. After about twelve minutes, eight vitamin pills appeared from somewhere. The bottle was still sealed tightly, and there was no sign that anything on it had been disturbed. Evidently, the eight pills were from the bottle, but they must have come out too fast, so the four of us observing it didn't have a chance to see where they came from. When they fell on the table, we did hear a light dropping sound.

After the vitamin pills came out, Yao Zheng smiled and said she had finished. I have heard EHF researchers say that when the pills don't come out, EHF demonstrators feel upset and frustrated, and sometimes they even sweat on their foreheads.

In our conversation, her father told of how the news media and the general public discovered Yao Zheng's EHF. He said that on July 2, 1990, students in Tianjin's Dagu Middle School were taking a test. Yao Zheng was concentrating and trying to answer the questions, when suddenly smoke started rising from her back. In an instant, two holes burned in her dress. All the other students and the teacher riveted their eyes to the scene. Afterward, the school reported this incident to the local bureau of education. When the story spread, a reporter from Tianjin City's *Chinese Journal of Petroleum* immediately came and reported on it.

Paul Dong and Thomas Raffill

Yao Zheng's father, Yao Wenji, is an engineer with the Tanggu District, Tianjin City, office of Bohai Oil Corporation, employed in that company's petroleum research laboratory, and her mother, Wang Lei, is a doctor in the pediatrics department of the same company's employee clinic. Her father told me about an inexplicable thing. When Yao Zheng first started to have EHF, about every ten days she would have an episode of giving off electricity and fire. Before this happened, the rims of her eyes would have black markings. Once, when the rims of her eyes had turned black, she petted a little rabbit. The rabbit had spasms and then died. Yao Zheng was very upset at the time. When she put her hand on a blank sheet of paper, the Chinese character for *rabbit* was burned into the paper. Another time, the sign appeared that she was about to have an EHF experience, her palm became hot, and it burned a yin-yang tai chi circle on a blank sheet of paper, although Yao Zheng had never seen one before. Would it be possible to infer that her father or mother had seen a yin-yang circle and the image was passed to her by thought? We can only conjecture.

In the two days I lived in their home, I saw her break a spoon by thought power. There was a sound when it broke. Then, I gave her the spoon I had brought to test her. Perhaps because the spoon was too solid, it didn't break, although it was bent by mind power. More surprisingly, it was transported to another place before it was bent. What happened was this: We were all concentrating on the spoon, but nothing happened for a long time. I saw she seemed to be struggling, so I called off the demonstration. After this, we all started talking about other things. Not long afterward, her father discovered that the spoon, which had been put on a tea table, was gone. We looked for it, and it turned up somewhere else in the room. When I found it, the spoon was bent.

CHINA'S SUPER PSYCHICS

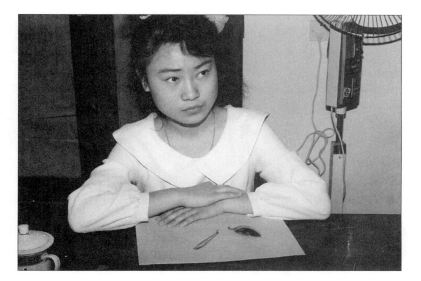

Fig. 11–2
Yao Zheng breaks a soup spoon by EHF. It made a noise when it broke.

In my experience of psychic matters, I have found that when you are concentrating on an object, nothing happens to it, but as soon as you pay a little less attention, perhaps for a microsecond, or a nanosecond, the object flies away. Chinese researchers have shown that in this phenomenon, which they call "unobservable flight," we cannot see its motion with the naked eye. Some people even believe that the flight of UFOs is a type of "unobservable flight."

Yao Zheng's parents told me that she can also open flowers. The following morning, her father and I went out to a nearby flower garden and picked some rosebuds and other flower buds for her to demonstrate with. She took the flowers and put them in her cupped hands. Then, she shook them by the side of her head. Soon she said the flowers had opened. When she opened her hands, the roses were in full bloom.

After she had opened flowers twice, I suggested that I

Paul Dong and Thomas Raffill

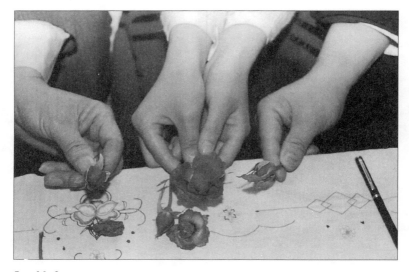

Fig. 11–3
Yao Zheng, uses her mind power to make a flower bud open. This demonstration
was witnessed by three magazine editors, along with Paul Dong. His hand is
shown at left.

could send chi to her head to see if this would make her open
flowers faster. She nodded in agreement, so I gathered my
chi in the palm and sent it to the top of her head. Soon she
felt full of energy, and then the flower bloomed. She told us
that when I sent chi to her, the flowers opened more easily.
When her mother asked me the reason, I told her that I had
been practicing chi gong for twenty years, and I could send
my energy out. Her mother asked me to show this, so I sent
chi to her palm. She felt a sensation of an electric current
flowing through her whole body.

After several more flower-opening demonstrations, I suggested doing another trial of removing pills from bottles, but
this time using the inflammation pills I had brought. Her father looked reluctant, but I explained to him, "For the last
two days, Yao Zheng has been demonstrating her EHF to us

Fig. 11–4
Two flowers were opened by Yao Zheng's mind power. The flower buds were picked from the nearby garden by Paul Dong.

and hasn't made any mistakes. This shows her abilities are moving in the right direction. Today, she has opened flowers many times. Her powers are at their peak, and she can't make any mistakes now." Her father thought this sounded reasonable, so he indicated to Yao Zheng to start a new demonstration.

After taking the bottle of medicine pills, she lightly shook it, sometimes stroking it with her hands, and mostly concentrating her mind on the bottle. Suddenly, eleven white pills came out. One of them was crushed. Our attention was captured by this one pill. Why was only one crushed? Was it smashed by falling on the table, or by "overcoming spatial obstacles" passing through the bottle? We were led to ponder a whole series of questions.

Because Yao Zheng's powers of starting a fire were especially strong, I was hoping to have a chance to see it. But her mother said that her combustion power had been suppressed

Fig. 11–5
Eleven white pills come out of the bottle (center); one of them smashed.

for several months and they didn't want it to start again. She explained, "If the burning power keeps coming out, she will burn all her clothes and it will be too expensive to take care of it. She was especially upset when she burned one of her pretty dresses."

She told me that Yao Zheng's fire-burning power was first discovered on the morning of December 7, 1989. That time, a part of her bedsheets were burned. After that, they often found burn holes in her clothes, socks, pants, sleeves, covers, gloves, and so on. The holes were generally one to ten centimeters in diameter, and more in the lower half and the back of her clothes. The strange thing about it is that her underclothes have avoided being burned, and there have been no signs of burn injury or pain.

"Who suppressed her fire-burning ability for her?" I asked.

CHINA'S SUPER PSYCHICS

"Someone from the Institute of Aerospace Medico-Engineering," she replied, not naming him. But I had an idea who it was. Yao Zheng later told me that the ones who taught her to suppress her fire were Professor Song Kongzhi of the Institute of Aerospace Medico-Engineering and Professor Chen Songliang of Beijing University's Institute of Life Sciences.

As I was beginning this book, I received *Chinese Journal of Somatic Science*, volume 2, 1994, with an article, "The Transformation of Uncontrollable EHF to Controllable EHF." The authors were Zhai Chengxiang and Professor Song Kongzhi. The former is the new leader of the government research programs in human body EHF research (replacing Zhang Zhenghuan, mentioned earlier), and the latter we have already encountered in chapter 5. The main idea of this article is that there are two kinds of EHF, controllable and uncontrollable. A year before encountering Yao Zheng, Professor Song Kongzhi discovered another person with uncontrollable EHF (he did not give the name). This is why he had the experience to help Yao Zheng with her uncontrollable EHF of burning clothes.

First, they taught her a simple control technique, which she was to practice herself at home. However, because she didn't practice hard, the effects were negligible. One day, November 6, 1990, Yao Zheng had an episode of uncontrollable burning, setting fire to the school dormitories, curtains, and some students' school supplies. The school asked her to withdraw, and wouldn't reregister her. She was facing expulsion from school. Then, her parents again requested the Institute of Aerospace Medico-Engineering to help with this problem. She stayed there fifty-six days, and since then, she has suppressed her burning power.

As mentioned above, Yao Zheng's father is an engineer

with the research department of Bohai Oil Company, a famous company in China. Could this be the reason Yao Zheng has developed the power to see oil under the ground? In 1994, accompanied by a Chinese oil-prospecting team, she discovered underground water and oil resources in the region of Ikezhaomeng in Inner Mongolia. A recent letter from her says that when she is in a good mood, she has more powers, such as seeing inside people's bodies, determining the sex of a fetus, finding stones and tumors in people, and so on.

As I mentioned earlier, my favorite EHF power is opening flowers. Everyone loves flowers, but I have been fortunate enough to see a demonstration of opening flowers, and the one who opened them is my friend. With regard to this, here is a previously unreported piece of information. In 1992, the Tianjin City Human Body Science Institute held a demonstration of "flower opening" and "removing pills from a bottle" as an entertainment event for visiting executives from U.S. oil companies. The demonstrator of opening flowers was Yao Zheng. The other, who demonstrated removing pills from bottles, was also female, but I don't know her name.

There are many people with the ability to open flowers in China, and Yao Zheng is only one example. Of course, there are others whose powers are stronger. On the evening of April 1, 1994, in the Beijing Signal Corps auditorium, Colonel Fu Songshan was able to open all of the flower buds in the hands of an audience of over a thousand people within thirty minutes. (I have a photograph of this event, but cannot reprint it here because of copyright restrictions.) However, Fu Songshan is not the top man. There is one mysterious woman who, facing thousands upon thousands of flower buds, can make them all bloom instantly by saying, "I want you all to open," and waving her hand.

After I returned to the U.S., Yao Zheng sent me some pages

CHINA'S SUPER PSYCHICS

Fig. 11–6
High-ranking executives of a U.S. oil company are watching Yao Zheng open a flower bud with her mind power. The young lady next to her is removing pills from a bottle by EHF. The photo was taken in Beijing, 1992.

from her diary of 1989–1991. These excerpts record the occasions when Yao Zheng had EHF episodes. I have deleted the parts already described above to avoid repetition. The rest of them are recorded here as reference material. I strongly believe that Yao Zheng will have more powerful EHF in the future. She is a young lady with great prospects in the area of EHF, and she may become one of the top super psychics in the future. She and her father have told me that she is willing to go abroad for scientific research purposes. If anyone would like to contact her or to see some of China's super psychics, I can act as an intermediary. Please write to Paul Dong, P.O. Box 2011, Oakland, CA 94604 U.S.A.

Paul Dong and Thomas Raffill

Fig. 11–7
Giving an EHF demonstration before an audience of hundreds, Yao Zheng produces golden spirit light as she releases her energy. Later, many audience members will find their diseases cured. Many people with EHF in China produce such pillars of light. Paul Dong has seen this three times.

1989

12/7 7:00 A.M. Woke up, discovered that a corner of the sheets (cotton) were burned.

12/9 Sleeves of nylon undergarment burned. Hole burned in right stocking.

12/11 10:30 P.M. Holes burned in red nylon undergarment.

12/14 Hole burned in bottom of socks, hole in corner of wool knit pants.

12/16 8:30 A.M. In school, blue sparks jumped from left hand. Around one to four sparks fell on a piece of paper and burned little holes the size of a grain of rice. Parts not burned through, just turned yellow.

12/17 7:00 P.M. Small hole burned in right pants pocket (made of cloth).

12/19 1:05 P.M. Lower right of cotton undershirt and nylon pants burned. Smoke, burning smell present. Diameter of hole in clothes ten cm.

3:00 P.M. Hole burned in lower right of undershirt. Heard piercing sound at the same time. Hard to stand it. Noise went away in an hour.

12/28 Before going to sleep, put New Year's cards and fountain pen on shelf at end of bed and tried a test of writing greetings by mind power. Went to sleep. Woke up several times to continue testing. Went to sleep. Woke up and found a partially completed Chinese character *zeng* ("gift to") written, without having touched the pen. The pen was lying on the floor, its cap was unopened. The handwriting and ink were just like mine.

1990

1/4 1:30 P.M. When shopping, burned a hole one cm in diameter in paper money.

4:15 p.m. Felt drowsy in class. Several holes burned in right sock. Felt alert again.

1/5 4:00 P.M. Held two coins in hand one hour pressed together. The point of contact had black spots and brown thready thing.

1/6 At morning class, exercise book disappeared. Contents of desk all gone.

1/7 4:00 P.M. Missing exercise book reappeared. Suddenly turned up on top of desk.

1/11 Walking on the street after school, suddenly felt dizzy. Everything went blank. I felt the power was coming on. I grabbed a New Year card with my hand. After it was burned, I returned to normal.

1/14 At school, I lost my key. Suddenly, I felt it was in the rice pot. I did find it there.

1/30 Used non-visual sensing to read the character for "horse."

1/31 I was holding a glass cup and it burst. There were little air bubbles in the water.

2/8 A plastic toy (deer) at home was standing on the bookshelf. In the afternoon, found it moved to the floor in front of the bookcase by itself.

2/9 Thermos bottle on shelf in kitchen moved into washing machine in bathroom. At the time, the doors were closed and the top of the washing machine was shut.

2/14 At 12:30 noon, found that the water thermos had moved from the kitchen shelf to the vegetable cleaning basket (it was standing upright).

2/16 At noon, found a lamp that had been on the writing desk before moved to the floor. The electric wire was pulled tight, but the plug was still in the socket.

2/25 The power came this afternoon and I broke the handle of a cup.

3/2 In first class this morning, found the books all gone from book bag. Only thing left was one of my sweatshirts. Went home to find the missing books. They were scattered all over the room.

3/29 Cloudy weather. At 10:00 A.M., burned holes in both socks. Threw them on the bed. At 7:15 P.M., found the burned socks were completely restored, with no trace of damage.

4/2 At noon, discovered that vegetable knife was missing. Found at 1:00 in washing machine in bathroom.

4/16 6:20 A.M. Clock in the house set itself back three hours.

4/17 In the afternoon, quartz watch hands were back one hour. Didn't see it happening, only saw the result.

CHINA'S SUPER PSYCHICS

5/3 Heard unbearable ear-splitting noise.

6/7 Burned up a pair of socks.

7/22 Rained in the morning. White rabbit that I had thrown out a week earlier suddenly appeared before my eyes. Threw it out again (put it in an iron cage).

7/27 Iron cage with rabbit moved back to the balcony.

10/10 Suffering from stomach pains. Doctor diagnosed it as appendicitis, treated it conservatively by antibiotics. Didn't help. At 10:00 A.M. on the 13th, sitting on blanket, burned a hole in it. The pain of appendicitis disappeared right away.

11/4 At 3:00 in the afternoon, succeeded in reading character "sun" without use of eyes. Took eighteen minutes. 10:30–11:30 at night, succeeded in reading letter "A," took an hour. Over the two months of trying to read with non-eye senses, some success and some failure. Also was able to remove pills from bottles three times over this period.

1991

1/15 Pill removal successful (removing pills from tightly sealed glass bottle). Three pills came out.

1/17 Pill removal successful. Moved seven pills. Took ten minutes. So far, able to remove 24 pills from bottle. Also testing out-of-body travel. During this, still sometimes lose control once in a while. But phenomena of burning clothes, etc. have not come back. Success rate at reading characters has fallen, but fairly high rate of success in tests of moving pills (through spacial barriers). Repeatability of experiments not good. Success rates from 30–50 percent.

Fig. 11–8
Yao Zheng (center) with a super psychic lady, Zhao Qunxue (right). At left is one of their leaders Zhai Yan Xiang.

The Heaven-Gifted Miracle Doctor Zhao Qunxue

I became acquainted with miracle doctor Zhao Qunxue at the introduction of Yao Zheng. The Defense Ministry in Beijing has a department of "Defense Science," and Zhang Baosheng, Yan Xin, Zhao Qunxue, and others are all VIPs in that department and are under government protection. Since Yao Zheng was discovered, she also goes there often to take part in experiments. She spends a lot of time with Zhao Qunxue. The difference in their ages is such that they could be mother and daughter, and Yao Zheng calls her Aunt Zhao. Because Yao Zheng is pretty, she is popular and many EHF people like her. For this reason, Yao Zheng's EHF has progressed greatly.

In the earlier section discussing the training of psychic children, one of the techniques given is to let them spend time around others with EHF powers, and in this way stimulate the growth of the EHF. This is the reason Yao Zheng has so many different types of power. She once wrote to me saying, "Aunt Zhao really likes me! She wants to increase my powers." She also often says that Zhang Baosheng is helping her develop higher powers. At first, Yao Zheng didn't have any healing abilities, but since she has had the spirit light (a yellow glow around the head when she uses her powers), she can cure many diseases. These abilities may have been given her by Aunt Zhao.

Zhao Qunxue is called "the Miracle Doctor of Guizhou" (Guizhou is a province in China). Toward evening on October 1, 1976, three fireballs appeared in the sky. They floated in the air with a blazing light that could be seen for miles around. People stared at them in amazement. Some called this a "spirit light," some said it was a UFO, some said it was a meteorite, and some said it was a part of a rocket falling back to earth. People soon forgot about it, but after Zhao Qunxue encountered this "spirit light," she inexplicably lost her mind. With her hair in a mess, she wandered aimlessly all around, and sometimes she stared at people passing by, giving warnings that they were going to get sick at a certain time, or that some accident was going to happen in their home in a few days and they should be very careful . . . and so on. Although it sounded crazy, all her predictions came true. As the stories multiplied and spread from person to person, soon she had turned into a local "miracle woman."

Although she was hailed as a miracle woman, people were not comfortable with her condition of mental illness. Four months later, her mental state returned to normal. One day, a neighbor's little boy was crying inconsolably. She gave him a hug, and he stopped crying. There is nothing strange about this, but the boy's stomach was aching badly, and when she touched his stomach, it stopped aching. How can this be explained? Also, how could it be explained that she was able to help people with everyday complaints like headaches, sprains, nosebleeds, and so on, just by touching them? Since Zhao Qunxue had this marvelous healing ability, her neighbors suggested that she start her own healing practice, earning money to repay what she had borrowed when she built her home. After discussing this with her husband, she opened her office the next day. When the news spread, it turned out that many people needed healings from her. As time went on, her family went from poverty to wealth. But then, disaster struck.

On April 29, 1980, *Guizhou Daily* published an account reporting that to earn money to repay a home construction loan, Zhao Qunxue was engaged in fraudulent practice of medicine without proper training, and was taking advantage of feudal superstitions, pretending to have spirit powers to swindle people of their money. She was given a light sentence because she was a first offender and confessed to her crimes, and she was sent to prison.

A Chinese proverb says, *"When the old country man lost his horse, how could he tell if it was bad luck or good?"* This means a loss may lead to a larger gain in the future. Because she was jailed, Zhao Qunxue later became a national treasure under government protection. It turned out that there were many sick people in the prison, and she cured all of them. When the guards and officials heard of this, they all wanted her to give healings for themselves and their families. Again, she cured all of them. Then, the jailers reported this to higher authorities. After they reviewed the evidence, they released her immediately and brought her to a national defense research center in Beijing. From then on, she came under "government protection."

Zhao Qunxue frequently does healings for top government officials. She usually mixes tea leaves with her hand, then tells her patients to pour water on it and drink. This tea has spirit power, and drinking it brings healing. When she stirs the tea leaves with her hand, people often see a bluish light coming from her hands. I would like to add that when we were in Yao Zheng's home watching her demonstrate opening flower buds, one of the journalists in the group saw a bluish light coming from Yao Zheng's hand. I have a very high regard for this bluish light, since it is a spirit light.

Of course, the amazing story of Zhao Qunxue does not end at this. As Hong Kong newspaper *Ming Pao* columnist A Le has disclosed, when Zhao Qunxue was in the Defense Ministry, she took part in an experiment on finding escaped prisoners by using her powers of remote viewing, and she was able to find the location of the prisoner. Zhao Qunxue's predictions are also amazingly accurate. She has done many readings using people's names to determine their character, health conditions, loyalty, and so on.

Li Lianjie, a star in China's martial arts world, once suffered from a strange illness. The skin of his stomach had swelled, he had difficulty eating, and was constipated. This made him feel a lack of physical strength and energy. Later, hospital X rays showed that his internal organs were in disarray, not in their normal places. Large and small intestines had tangled around his stomach and liver. As he himself admitted, he sometimes put his body through contortions during martial arts fighting, and this might be the cause of the trouble. But he was afraid to undergo major surgery. Later, at the introduction of Zhang Baosheng, he requested the healing services of Zhao Qunxue. She felt his stomach with her hands a few times, and the disease was cured. When asked how she cured Li Lianjie's illness, she replied that she probably pushed his organs into the right place by rubbing his stomach. When our stomach hurts, it is natural to rub it with our hands. The difference is that her hand gives off the blue light and is a wonder hand.

To this day, I still have several samples of the "spirit tea" imbued with Zhao Qunxue's blue light that she sent me. If anyone would like to do experiments with it, I would be glad to provide some.

A Modern Magician—Zhang Yansheng

You may say Zhang Yansheng is the best fortune teller. He has a sensitivity to body energy which he uses for diagnosing people's diseases. He was born in Shandong Province. He graduated from the Beijing Aeronautics Institute, and after practicing chi gong over a prolonged period, he discovered that he had the skill of diagnosing diseases by reading palms, and was even able to diagnose people at long distances. After he became famous, people called him "a modern-day magician."

Here's an example of Zhang Yansheng in action. A woman asked Yansheng to read her palm. Yansheng had never met this woman before, but after taking a look at her palm, he told her that three or four days earlier she had a fight with her husband.

At this, the woman looked uncomfortable. Some companions who had come with her were struggling to suppress their laughter. It turned out that her present husband worked in the diplomatic service and had been abroad for over a year.

However, she had just had a meeting with her ex-husband, and she did get into a fight with him. She was highly embarrassed to have this whole story come out from the palm-reading like this.

How does he do it? Zhang Yansheng is extremely sensitive to body energy. On one occasion, for example, Yansheng visited a friend. As soon as he got through the door, he felt uncomfortable. He searched around in the room, looking for an object with "mystic energy." Finally, he found a Buddhist statue, and he cried out excitedly, "That's it!" The statue had collected over a hundred years' worth of energy released by lamas meditating before it, and this energy had not dissipated—it remained stored in the statue. Ordinary people cannot sense this kind of energy, but people who have attained success in their chi gong practice can sense it very clearly.

The reader may find it hard to understand this story, so let us look at it from another angle. Suppose a person has practiced chi gong for five years or more and attained some power at it. Suppose, further, that he wears the same clothes every time he practices chi gong and he never washes these clothes. These clothes would then collect the chi (energy) released during his chi gong practice. Now suppose his child catches a cold one day. He has the child put on these clothes. The child will get over the cold twice as fast as usual, because human body energy is most effective against colds. I have practiced chi gong for over twenty years and have had this experience—that makes it easier to understand the airy-sounding story about the Buddhist statue.

I have some experiences which are very good examples to illustrate this situation. In 1993, I taught a chi gong class of thirty-two students for the San Francisco College of Acupuncture. Most of the students tried on my energy jacket, and all said they felt the chi. In 1995, I held a chi gong class in

Paul Dong and Thomas Raffill

the state of Oregon for twenty-eight students. Out of the class, twenty-six of them said my jacket had chi. More recently, sociology professor Deborah Woo asked me to lecture on "the concept of chi" to her class of fifty at the University of California at Santa Cruz. Only two of the students said they didn't feel anything in my chi-imbued jacket. This demonstrates the fact that chi can accumulate in an object.

Zhang Yansheng's friend had brought that statue back from a trip to Tibet. A lama gave it to him and said it was a Buddhist protective spirit, the kind of statue which Buddhists place in large numbers inside their temples. The lamas meditated before it every day, and over the years it accumulated the chi of the lamas. What is more, the chi of the lamas is different from ordinary chi, because their meditation produces a strong radiant chi, while ordinary chi is nonradiant. This chi is a force which has healing properties.

Zhang Yansheng's palm-reading is nothing unusual; there are palm readers everywhere in the world. What *is* unusual is the ability to read a person's palm to tell the fortune of the person's relatives. On one occasion, a magazine reporter interviewed Zhang Yansheng. After examining the reporter's hand, Yansheng pronounced that within three days his wife would have an ailment of the shoulder. The reporter paid no attention to this, because his wife had never had any shoulder problems before. But three days later, sure enough, his wife actually did suffer a strong pain in the shoulder and had to go to the hospital.

The reporter was mystified. He came back for a second interview and said he understood how Zhang could diagnose a person's disease by looking at his palm, because a person's palm might show some symptoms of the disease inside his body. But he wondered how Zhang could explain the ability to look a someone's palm and diagnose his *relative's* diseases.

"Oh, that's the information-transfer effect," said Yansheng with great confidence. After living together for a prolonged period, the man and his wife developed an information interchange, and his and his wife's information must be reflected in their hands.

Zhang Yansheng shared some of his thoughts about this effect with the reporter. Chinese scientists have found out that the etherial substance in the body which Chinese traditional medicine calls chi is actually an energy flow, an information carrier. Chi gong, the form of meditation which has been so popular in mainland China lately, allows a person who has practiced the exercise for a certain period of time to guide the chi inside his body outward. Even people who have never practiced chi gong also emit some chi, but so faintly that only very sensitive or psychic people can feel it. This is also the basis for fortune-telling and medical diagnosis by astrology, magic, and spiritual readings, except that there are some fakes who have no psychic powers and who use these practices as a false front to cheat people of their money.

A friend of the reporter who had overheard this piece of conversation became quite curious, and he thrust out his right hand and asked Zhang Yansheng to do a reading of his wife's health. Zhang Yansheng concentrated on the man's palm.

"For the past two days, your wife has been in an unfamiliar environment, and she has a skin allergy," he said.

The friend exclaimed, "That's true! Last night my wife made a long-distance telephone call to me. She said she isn't comfortable with the southern climate and food, and she has come down with an allergy." He explained that his wife had been assigned to work on Hainan Island. He was astonished that Yansheng could read her symptoms from 1,200 miles away.

Zhang Yansheng explained, "Long-distance readings have

Paul Dong and Thomas Raffill

a simple explanation. Everybody has an energy field, and everybody's field is different, in the same way that everybody's fingerprint is different. All you need to do is mention a person's name, or let me talk on the telephone with the person, or let me see a word written by the person, in short give me a small amount of the person's information, and it's just like tuning in a radio to the right frequency—I can read what's happening to the person."

Where do Zhang Yansheng's strange powers come from? His powers are not inborn, but were developed by practicing chi gong. We must admit that inborn powers are not always stronger than those developed through training, nor are powers developed through training always better than inborn powers. To be fair, both inborn and trained powers have their advantages.

The Great Master of Universal Language—Chen Letian

Master Chen Letian is one of the new generation of EHF people in mainland China, particularly famous in the area around the cities of Shanghai and Hangzhou. After he became famous, he was naturally invited abroad to teach and heal. After traveling through Japan and Europe, he has come to San Francisco, U.S.A. I met him in San Francisco.

The first time we met, we were already like old friends. In mainland China, he often read *The Journal of UFO Research*, a bimonthly publication (circulation 320,000) of Gansu Province People's Publishing House, for which I served as senior editor. He, like many people involved in psychic matters in China, likes to read UFO magazines. Those who have developed EHF tend to report having more contact with UFOs. They are convinced that psychic phenomena and UFOs or

CHINA'S SUPER PSYCHICS

Fig. 11–9
Master Chen Letian demonstrates his healing abilities before a crowd of students in San Francisco.

extraterrestrials are in some way related. People in the U.S. and European UFO research communities share this impression. We are close to a worldwide consensus on this issue. The first day I met Master Chen, he invited me to be a consultant for the Tian Gong Research Society. Tian gong is a meditation practice invented by him. It was through the practice of tian gong that he developed EHF.

I have read a book entirely about him, and seen a video documentary of his work. I have also attended some of his lectures and twice went to his "lecture with emitted chi" in San Francisco. I am quite familiar with him and know how strong his powers are.

Once he told me there was a woman professor who had suffered from severe headaches for seven years. She had tried many treatments with no success. After taking his chi gong class and going to his "lectures with emitted chi" three times, she was cured of the headaches she had been suffering from for seven years. I checked this once, sitting next to the lady professor and asking her about the headaches. She confirmed that she was cured. The wife of a friend of mine went to him because of her severe fatigue. After three healings from him, she had an 80 percent improvement in her condition. Of course, I have also interviewed many of his students (most students join his classes because they have health problems). Over half of them said they were getting good results.

As his consultant, I often visit his office. He has a few ladies assisting him because they studied under him and received benefits. Out of gratitude and admiration, they are glad to help him in his work. One of the ladies, a woman from mainland China who does not wish to be identified, is said to be able to see everything in the office from her home. Another, Ms. Chen Meifang, is the manager of a sewing company. She suffered from vinitis, stomach ailments, and heart disease. At first, she did not believe in chi gong and was uncomfortable with psychic claims. Only because her conditions were so serious did she come to Master Chen's lecture with emitted chi, with the idea of just giving it a try. She felt very comfortable for the whole two hours. She was surprised. Could it be a psychological effect?

After the lecture, she bought a souvenir imbued with Master Chen's chi. Such items (souvenirs, posters, calendars, cards, et cetera) are said to have healing and protective abilities, which sounds like a superstition. But the strange thing was that her vinitis was getting better. So, she decided to join his chi gong class. When she went to class, she first wanted to meet Master Chen to tell him that the vinitis she had suffered from for many years was healing. When she met him, Master Chen gestured his hand toward her nose and sent some chi to it. She says her vinitis was cured completely by that.

Her stomach and heart conditions gradually improved as she practiced his system of exercises. What was even more fortunate for her was that she experienced the *bi gu* or psychic fasting phenomenon. Since then, she has gone for several months without eating. She has said that she gave up meat on March 16, 1996, and after that gave up fried foods. Then, she stopped eating anything and only drinks a little water. As of the time I interviewed her, November 2, 1996, she had gone over seven months without eating.

She told me that at first, her mother and husband were against this, but since going without food has not affected her physical and mental strength, and the conditions of her illnesses are improving every day, her husband has had nothing to complain about and is not trying to stop her.

This story spread to a dentist. It may have been through a friend of hers who knew the dentist. One day, she went to have her tooth removed. But the dentist refused to treat her, because she hadn't had anything to eat or drink for months and he was afraid she wouldn't be able to withstand the treatment. She was forced to look for another dentist she didn't know to extract the tooth. This experience reminded her of a Chinese folk saying: *"Tell people only part of what you know; don't reveal all that you are thinking."*

I have seen Chen Meifang's fasting myself. At 5:00 P.M. on November 2, 1996, I met her in Master Chen's office. At 6:00 she, Master Chen, and I went out to have dinner. Ms. Chen ordered for us. She picked three dishes and soup. The first thing the waitress said to her was, "You won't be having anything to eat again today?" She smiled and nodded. It turned out that she came there often.

When the food came, I saw it was prepared excellently and smelled great. But she still didn't take a bite of it. She looked very relaxed and didn't show any signs of envying us for eating so well. I don't think she was pretending. She had nothing to gain from that.

Another middle-age lady, Ha Toi Chun, is a business-woman from Hong Kong who often travels between Hong Kong, Taiwan, and the U.S. on business. I am more familiar with her, and have had lunch with her three times, all at her invitation and at her expense. The first time, we went to a teahouse (a Cantonese dim sum restaurant) for lunch. She ordered seven or eight delicious dim sum items, but she didn't eat a bite herself. I asked her why, and Master Chen answered for her. "She has been fasting for half a year."

"She doesn't eat anything at all?" I asked.

"I don't feel well when I eat, but I feel fine when I don't," she said.

I am deeply familiar with the psychic fasting phenomenon, so I only asked her that one question. Another time we had lunch, she took us to a high-class restaurant in Chinatown. Prices were high, and we ordered five dishes for the three of us. Again, she didn't eat anything. I tested her by saying, "How about having a little?" She just shook her head. Perhaps Master Chen wanted to display his powers. He picked up a piece of food with his chopsticks and gave it to her, saying, "Have it." She did eat it. Then, I asked her, "Aren't you afraid you won't be feeling well?" Master Chen answered this, saying she had nothing to be afraid of if he told her to eat it.

You may have wondered how he could use his own chop-sticks to give food to her. As a master with special powers, he is said to be able to disinfect things by concentrating on them. About twelve years earlier, when I made my first trip to mainland China to investigate chi gong and EHF, I met Tan Yaoxiang, a chi gong master from Guangxi Province. He washed his clothes in a tub of dirty water, then took a needle out of his pocket and stuck it in his patient's leg. I asked him how he could use that water that many people had washed their hands in without fear of spreading infection. He said, "I disinfected it with my mind." Before he used the needle, I saw him wave his fingers over it a few times. He was probably using his external chi to disinfect it.

The last time Ms. Ha took us out, we went to a dim sum restaurant. We again ordered all kinds of dim sum dishes, and she didn't touch any of it, or even drink tea. She said that since she started fasting, she had lost twenty pounds (she had been overweight), but she felt as strong as ever, was neither fatigued nor sleepless, and the six months of fasting had got rid of her diseases. She also seemed to be full of energy. Also, I am convinced it was real, because they wouldn't gain anything by going to such elaborate lengths to fool me about such a thing. They just ask me some things about San Francisco once in a while. Besides, psychic fasting is not unique with her. There are many such fasters in mainland China. The longest fast, by one of Yan Xin's students, has gone on for six years.

I often talk with Master Chen Letian. He particularly recommended to me one of his students, a sixty-seven-year-old woman from mainland China. Her name is Zou Benlan and she a pediatrician from the city of Qingdao in Shandong Province. On March 15, 1995, she went to the city of Hangzhou. The West Lake of Hangzhou is one of the most famous tourist attractions in China, and is considered a must-see for both Chinese and international travelers. It is about three hours by train from Shanghai. Zou Benlan went there to study tian gong (Master Chen Letian's chi gong practice). On the fourth day, she developed a painting EHF. In the Chinese EHF community, this phenomenon is called "chi gong paintings." She just picks up a brush and it turns into a painting instantly, without conscious thought on her part. She wants to paint all day, including pen drawings, Chinese inkbrush paintings, watercolors, and oils. But she had never studied painting. By June 1996 she had completed over 2,000 works, no two of them alike. A professor at the Beijing Academy of Art loved her chi gong paintings and asked her to make seventy for a "chi gong exhibition."

Zou Benlan's paintings are not only beautiful, but also have healing powers. Many people who have received paintings from her have been cured. Of course, not all are cured, but it is clear that the connection between the paintings and the recoveries is no coincidence. This type of effect from an EHF information signal is known in other cases as well. For example, some people are cured of their diseases by viewing videos of Yan Xin's lectures with emitted chi. This is the same thing, although you might consider it a "psychological effect."

Zou Benlan is convinced that her ability is a Heaven-sent gift, and so she wants to do good deeds. She is arranging to have a portion of the receipts from the sale of her paintings, after costs, donated to a charity called Hope Engineers. This is a recently established educational institution in China providing free primary education for poor children. Recently, she has done seventy-five watercolor and oil paintings and sent these, with photographs of them, to Master Chen. He let me pick three of them as a gift to me.

Zou Benlan is not the only person in China who can do chi gong painting. I often read news reports of people who have attained "chi gong painting" or "chi gong calligraphy" skills through their meditation practice. China has many psychics with diverse abilities, as if someone in the air spread sparkles to make the world a more beautiful place.

The multitalented Zou Benlan, besides her chi gong painting and healing, can also sing universal songs and speak universal language. I am not familiar with the former, but the latter is Master Chen's special healing technique. As Master Chen describes it, when he developed EHF through his chi gong practice, at the same time he learned a kind of language. He himself does not know what it is, so he calls it *tian yu* (universal language). Maybe this is the language that ancient wizards used for their spells. He speaks it spontaneously when giving healings to people. The patient doesn't need to understand what it means, just hearing it is enough to help make the disease go away. Master Chen himself is not sure whether it is the universal language that cures the patient or if it is his mind power. To the patient, it doesn't make a difference, as long as he is cured. An idea worth considering is that when Master Chen uses universal language in doing healings, the patient is covered with this beautiful and mysterious sound, and as a result will be more focused and relaxed, and the effects of the treatment will be better.

Master Chen has spoken universal language to me. One time, using spiritual writing, he dedicated a greeting card to me, wishing me "health, wisdom, peace, and success." It looks like a rapidly scribbled signature or a magic talisman. It is a pretty sight.

A Policewoman's Stunning Powers

In Beijing, there is a policeman called Li Denglai. Most people living in Beijing know that he has a terrifying power, but few people know that the super weapon he uses to win fights with criminals is water. He has practiced his skill for twenty years. The spray of water from his mouth has the force of a BB gun, but a BB gun can only shoot one pellet at a time, and these may miss their mark. But the water droplets spit out of the mouth make a thick spray of innumerable pellets, and there is no dodging them. The only defense for the criminal is to run away as fast as he can.

Li Denglai does not generally carry a gun or knife. The only thing he carries is a water bottle. People don't know what he uses it for. But if you know how he uses water, you won't dare try to make trouble in his range.

Then, does this mean that Li Denglai is the most powerful master? Perhaps not, because there is another who does not even use water. She wins fights with mind power alone! This is not a fictional account, but a well-established fact.

Since 1986, the military and police in all China's major cities, such as Beijing, Tianjin, Shanghai, and Guangzhou, have employed a number of top people with EHF powers. Their powers range from remote viewing, foreseeing the future, seeing through objects, or viewing through walls, opening locks, winding watches (resetting the times), moving objects . . . all the way to walking through walls. Aided by this EHF power, they have been able to solve their cases (or complete their missions) much more quickly, sometimes in as little as an hour.

As can easily be imagined, EHF plays an essential role in the military, aviation, technology and medicine, industries, and in national sports competitions. However, these are beyond the scope of our present discussion. In this section, we will focus only on Miss Sun Xiaogang, an EHF person in the city police of Zhengzhou.

CHINA'S SUPER PSYCHICS

Sun Xiaogang is twenty-six years old as of this writing. She was discovered to have EHF seventeen years ago when she saw a neighboring woman pass by. The woman was pregnant, and Sun stared with curiosity. As she focused on her, she learned that the child in her was a girl. This later turned out to be correct. In those days, she usually displayed such abilities as see-through vision and remote viewing. When she was fourteen years old, she was absent from class for a month due to illness. When the examination time came, the school expected her to make up the material she missed to prepare for the test. She had to study hard to catch up, but in the end she scored higher than anybody else, because she had precognition and knew what would be on the test in advance.

When news of all these strange powers of Sun Xiaogang's spread to national law enforcement agencies, she was assigned to work in the EHF Clinical Research Lab of Zhengzhou City Police Hospital, Henan Province. Once, Chen Wei, a reporter from Henan Province, was interviewing her and asked her to demonstrate the EHF power of making a nut and bolt screw themselves together. The reporter had brought a nut and bolt, which he placed in a glasses case, handing the case to Sun Xiaogang and shutting it. Then, Sun Xiaogang held the glasses case tightly and closed her eyes. In about a minute, Sun Xiaogang turned the case over, and there was a rolling sound in the case. But there was only the sound of one object, indicating that the two items were put together. Opening the case, they saw that the nut was screwed onto the bolt, but only halfway down. The reporter, Chen Wei, thought that was enough.

Sun Xiaogang also has the ability to cause flower buds to open, but this ability is too common and is nothing compared to making green fruit turn red. On a certain day in March 1990, a Shanghai television production crew came to Zhengzhou, Henan Province. They were producing a documentary on the unusual people and things of China, and the title, naturally enough, was *Amazing People and Things of China*.

As the scene opens, a law enforcement officer brings a bowl of unripe, green cherries, and Sun Xiaogang takes one and puts it in her right hand. At this time, hundreds of people are watching her right hand. After about three minutes, a smile appears on Sun's face. She opens her hand, and a completely ripe, red cherry appears before the audience! As a Chinese rhyme goes, *"Red cherries are ready, green bananas are green when ripe."*

Moving objects with the mind, or psychokinesis, is a very common type of EHF. This is nothing compared to restoring a broken leaf to its original form and shrinking it. The time was October 17, 1990, 7:00 A.M. The woman journalist Zhong Zhanghong came to Sun Xiaogang's residence. After seeing her perform many kinds of EHF, she asked her to let her see her ability to shrink leaves. After Sun agreed to this, the journalist went and picked a leaf from the garden, broke it into three pieces and gave it to Miss Sun. Sun pieced the leaf together, joining the pieces back where they were broken apart. Then, on a blank piece of paper, she drew a picture of a complete (unbroken) leaf, along with five more leaves, each smaller than the last one. Below this she wrote, *first rejoin then shrink, shrink,* and *change.* Also, at the bottom of the page, she wrote, *The mind has thought, thought becomes stronger, the leaf is restored, the leaf keeps its shape, the leaf's chlorophyll decreases.* Then, she pressed the leaves together in her hands. A minute and a half later, she said, "It is done," and opened her hands. At that moment, as the journalist describes it, she didn't dare to believe her eyes. Not only was the leaf restored, it was many times smaller than when it started, and was the size of a fingernail!

CHINA'S SUPER PSYCHICS

The reader may have noticed that these sentences such as *the leaf's chlorophyll decreases* don't quite seem to make sense. We can never tell what the psychic mysteries really mean. I suppose it means that if the chlorophyll is less, the leaf will get smaller. The psychic effect did not follow the words *the chlorophyll decreases* but the word *shrink*.

Sun Xiaogang's EHF is powerful, but the power that most pleases the law enforcement authorities is her ability to trace criminals from the clues they leave behind. One particularly interesting story about this took place in September 1988. Someone stole 100 yuan (Chinese currency) from her briefcase in the police residence halls. She lay on the bed silently for a moment, and then she thought of the scene when the person entered her room. A familiar form appeared in her mind's eye (perhaps from the traces of the person's information signals). She saw the figure go stealthily to the briefcase, open the cover, reach in . . . Oh, so she's who it was! Thinking to protect the reputation of the perpetrator, she was planning to persuade her nicely to return the money when she found her, saying she wouldn't tell anybody. But the thief denied it.

At that time, an idea flashed into her mind. "I remember now. Last night I got off work at eleven-forty, and you went in there at eleven-thirty and took my 100 yuan. It must be that you wanted to test my EHF, right?"

On hearing this, the woman instantly replied, "Comrade Xiaogang, everyone says your EHF is all-powerful, but I didn't believe in it. That's why I took your money with the purpose of testing your abilities. Now I'm convinced." Saying this, she immediately returned the money to Sun.

This lady with powerful EHF has used her special power of retrieving information from leftover traces to solve one case after another for the law enforcement authorities!

Sun Xiaogang is not the only EHF person this powerful in

Paul Dong and Thomas Raffill

the Zhengzhou police. Besides her, there are Guo Yanqin (twenty-two years old as of this writing) and Dong Hongxia (twenty-three years old). They are all women, and people call them "the three strange flowers." Each one is more powerful than the next. Guo Yanqin can see objects buried three feet underground and can make watches go faster or slower. If she says, "Go, go, go," to herself, the watch goes faster, and if she says, "Back, back, back," to herself, the watch sets itself back.

One time, she was asked to demonstrate the special ability of "retrieving a letter by mind power." After she was given a letter in an envelope that was sealed securely with glue, she put it between her hands and looked at the envelope from different angles, looking very confident. At the time, a member of the audience had on a mini radio that was broadcasting a weather forecast. A journalist in the audience motioned him to turn it off, but Guo Yangin said there was no need. A little while later, she suddenly cried out, "It's come, its come." Before the reporter knew what was happening, the page of the letter floated to the ground.

The journalist looked over the envelope and didn't see any signs of tearing. She had been observing the whole process carefully, and there had been no chance for her to play any tricks. The paper that came down was the journalist's writing, the four words *Tian Jin medical expert* in large Chinese characters. As the journalist was inspecting and pondering it, one of the other EHF ladies, Dong Hongxia, said, "No need to inspect it. This is EHF, you won't find anything. Just let me send the slip back into the envelope."

This suggestion was just what the reporter wanted. Getting the page out was hard enough, wouldn't it be even harder to put it back in? But Dong said she could do it. The only thing she asked was that the page be folded up. The journalist agreed but asked the reason. She said, "The piece of paper is too big. It would take me a long time to do it. If you fold it up, I can save a lot of time." So saying, Dong folded the paper a few times and placed it on top of the envelope, then pressed it between her hands. As she was doing this, she chatted with the others. In just ten minutes, the letter had got back into the envelope without anybody noticing. Checking the envelope, they found no signs that anything had been disturbed, but it was absolutely clear that the letter was inside.

When the journalist asked Miss Dong how she knew the letter had entered the envelope, she gave a surprising answer: "Whenever anything happened to the letter, it was transmitted from my hand to my mind. My mind is like a television screen, and can see it all clearly. But the scene flashed by instantly, and it would be hard to catch it even by high-speed photography."

Another of Miss Dong's specialties is her ability to read the words on any page in a book. All you need to do is tell her the page and line numbers, and she can read it as if it were right before her eyes. An even more astonishing EHF power is her ability to turn white hair black and to make a broken branch grow back. Wheat that she has handled will produce a higher and richer crop yield. One time, she mentioned that someone had a kumquat in the next room. A journalist asked her to demonstrate her power to move it. She sat up straight on the bench and concentrated her mind. In a few minutes, a kumquat came into her hand. When they checked the other room, the found there had been twenty-three kumquats and now there were only twenty-two left. The people who witnessed this clapped and cheered.

These three super-powerful ladies naturally aroused the interest of the National Security Agency. A research center conducted tests of their powers under strict controls. According to reports, there were many instruments such as they had never seen before, but the first test was to see an object in another room. Their results were "completely correct." One thing that occurs to me is that if they combine their powers, security vaults such as used by NASA in the U.S. to keep secret documents will not be safe from them.

Having read this, the reader need not be surprised. Don't forget that China has a population of 1.2 billion people, and among them we must find people with more and more amazing abilities. Miss Sun Chulin, born in the city of Wuhan in 1957 and now employed as an assistant researcher with the Human Body Science Laboratory of the Chinese University of Geology, can change the constitution of materials, and use this to produce the petroleum that is so vital to modern life. Master Li Lianyuan of Huizhou, Guangdong Province, giving a demonstration of moving objects with his mind to a high-ranking official of the Chinese Council of State, removed 10,000 dollars from a bank (China's foreign currency reserves now stand at 100 billion U.S. dollars).

You might be filled with admiration at the description of what these two can do, but you need not be too envious. There is a limit to everything in this universe. Sun Chulin can only make a small amount of petroleum. If she could produce a thousand barrels a day, her job title certainly would not be "assistant researcher." Instead she would probably be a chief engineer or executive in a Chinese oil company. As for Li Lianyuan's 10,000 dollars, they were not his to spend. The Chinese philosophy does not approve of taking tainted money. If you remove money from a bank, many people will suffer for it. It is not right to make a fortune on the suffering of others. Chinese Buddhists say that if you use unearned wealth, you will lose your powers. Nobody wants to do that. All he could do was use EHF to return the money to the bank.

CHINA'S SUPER PSYCHICS

Buddhist beliefs also claim that if a master uses his special powers to humiliate a woman, he will not only lose his powers but his descendants will suffer punishment for it. True or not, it is enough to make them cautious in their actions. Even if a person has special powers, there must be something that can stop it. This is a part of the Chinese philosophy that all things constrain each other, a truth that nobody can deny.

The Modern Guan Yin—the Supreme Power

Whether or not to believe in psychics is one question, the reliability of psychic powers is another, and whether or not there is a towering figure in the world of psychic masters is another. Before attempting to answer these questions, let us introduce two ancient characters whose names are household words in China, Ji Gong and Guan Shiyin, to give the reader the background on these historical authorities in China. A goddess of similar towering stature is alive today among the 1.2 billion people of China.

Yan Xin, as already related in chapter 6, has been called "the modern Ji Gong" by Chinese followers of psychic matters. Who, then, is Guan Shiyin?

About 2,500 years ago, there was a woman the Chinese called Guan Shiyin or Guan Yin. She was the daughter of an imperial prince of the first degree. It was said she turned her mind to Buddha, and this brought her special powers like EHF. She was more powerful than Ji Gong. The Buddhists describe this level as "the six spiritual penetrations," which include *divya-cakesus* (heavenly eye, "the penetration that sees things in the heavens"), *divya-srotra* (heavenly ear or the "penetration that hears things in the heavens"), *paracitta-jnana* ("the penetration that knows others' minds"), *purya-nivasanusmeti-jnana* ("the penetration that knows the past lives"), *rodhividhi-jnana* ("the penetration that traverses everywhere"), and *asravaksaya-jnana* ("the penetration that fills everything"). Guan Shiyin possessed all of these spiritual powers.

The heavenly eye has been described in chapter 10, but this heavenly eye is more like the dharma eye described there. "The penetration that traverses everywhere" refers to the ability to go through obstacles (as in Zhang Baosheng's ability to walk through walls). This includes the ability to transform oneself into a spirit and go anywhere, such as the skies or underground. "The penetration that knows others' minds" is like the ability of Zhang Yuji described below, to know what others are thinking—in other words, telepathy. Zhang Yuji also has "the penetration that knows past lives," and can tell the past and the future. "The penetration that fills everything" is the highest of the six penetrations, and only the immortals attained this level of power. Lord Buddha and Guan Shiyin are examples of such immortals, who had mastery of the whole world and could do anything.

Guan Shiyin was kind and benevolent. She liked to save people in trouble, and she always answered people's calls for help. That is why the Chinese people called her "Goddess of Mercy." When you face disaster, no matter where you may be, if you speak her name, she will respond and save you, because she has the heavenly ear and heavenly eye. That is why the people gave her the name of Guan Shiyin, which means "one who can detect any voice in the world, no matter how weak."

Besides Lord Buddha, Guan Shiyin is the most revered immortal in China. Any woman who has super-high EHF will be called a modern Guan Shiyin or a little Guan Shiyin. To my knowledge, China has had three women with EHF who have been called little Guanyins. One of these is a woman in

Fig. 11–10
The Goddess of Mercy, Guan Yin. Illustrations from John Stevenson, *Yoshitori:
One Hundred Aspects of the Moon*, San Francisco Graphic Society. Grateful Ac-
knowledgement is given to the publisher, Min Yee.

Shanxi Province, now thirty-two, named Zhang Yuji. She can tell the past and the future, make predictions in business, stocks, and people's fates with great accuracy. She has remote viewing powers which enable her to see into other people's homes, the arrangement of objects there, what the environment around looks like, and so on. She can also see how much money a person has in the bank, and she also has well-established abilities to see through people's bodies and diagnose their diseases. When asked why her powers are so extraordinary, she says that behind her is the Goddess of Mercy controlling her. The Chinese call this type of phenomenon "Guan Shiyin visiting the world." Once, at the invitation of a high-ranking official, she went to the city of Shenzhen, called "the little Hong Kong," a town between Hong Kong and Guangzhou which was undergoing rapid economic expansion at that time. Because the news was leaked, she was surrounded by the press and media.

Comparing Zhang Yuji with the Goddess of Mercy, there is an enormous difference. Simplistically speaking, perhaps the combined powers of Yan Xin, Zhang Baosheng, and Zhang Yuji can compare to those of the woman in mainland China today known only as "the modern Goddess of Mercy." We do not know her name, but only that she is a woman. This is in line with the tendency for China to have more women than men among the psychics. Speaking of her powers, some say she truly is a modern Guan Shiyin, a leading figure in EHF that towers over the multitudes.

The powers of the modern Guan Shiyin are so amazing as to be unbelievable. Also, the fantastic scope of her powers has made it hard to keep it secret. Suppose any country held a secret military presentation in which a person presented as a skilled magician burned himself to death and then reappeared on another part of the stage? The members of the audience would think it was so amazing, they would tell their wives, and they in turn would call their parents right away ... and in this way, the military secret will be leaked.

The main figure of this section has given just such a secret demonstration. The purpose of organizing this demonstration was to show how powerful she is, as a kind of show of authority over the people.

It is said that on an autumn evening, in an auditorium of some army base in northern China, hundreds of people with EHF from all parts of the country were gathered. Most of them were women. While they were waiting for the presentation to start, all the lights in the hall went out. Nobody knew why. If it was to show a movie, there was no screen or projector to be seen. As they were all starting to talk about this, a wave of delicate scent with something like sandalwood came to their noses. At this point, they saw a middle-aged woman announcer and a young lady come out. The older woman took to the podium and announced, "Everyone please close your eyes, clear your minds, and concentrate on meditation for fifteen minutes." Chi gong meditation was the specialty of these hundreds of EHF masters, so telling them to do meditation to strengthen their powers was just what they wanted to do. But usually they would keep going for an hour or more, so why were they being asked to do it for only fifteen minutes? This was another question mark in everyone's mind. But all they could do was follow the instructions.

No sooner had the fifteen minutes passed than the announcer said, "The meditation is concluded. Everyone please slowly open your eyes." When they opened their eyes, everyone turned their eyes toward the podium. They saw a shining halo around the head of the young lady, many times brighter than what you can see around most people in the dark. Later, people described her halo as almost like those portrayed in paintings of the Goddess of Mercy. The brighter a person's halo is, the stronger the power. This was as good as telling everyone there that she was the master of all masters. Her scent was still constantly spreading around. This scent was not coming from her clothes or her makeup, but from her aura. No other woman besides Yang Meiqun could give out such an enchanting scent, but Yang Meiqun was an elderly woman of ninety years old by this time. The person in this event appeared to be no older than twenty-six.

When this meeting of all the EHF people concluded, the young lady slowly departed, accompanied by the announcer, and the lights went on again. People felt compelled to look at their watches, and a strange thing happened. All of the hundreds of people's watches had stopped! Her scent, her halo, the stopping of all the watches, all these things told people that she was the top of Chinese EHF. Some people might still wonder, how would this be explained against the powers of Yan Xin, Zhang Baosheng, and all the other famous and powerful masters there? That is not difficult. The Chinese martial arts world has a saying, *"The real masters do not show themselves."* All of the most powerful people are unknown.

Someone told me another strange thing. When this modern goddess faced a field of flowers, she raised her hand toward them and all the flower buds opened. Not one flower bud had the temerity to go against her will. More amazingly, she can transfer her powers to another person, who can then use them on a third person, to confuse the people she is dealing with. This is a reappearance of the "thousand hands" technique used by the ancient Goddess of Mercy. "Thousand hands" refers to the diversification of the powers until they spread everywhere and do everything. The strange powers of the modern Goddess of Mercy are enough to make people's blood run cold.

• 12 •

How China's Skeptics Took Advantage of American Observers

"These Chinese claim super-psychic abilities, but their only ability is to disappear when asked to prove themselves." In words much like these, American skeptics of the psychic described Chinese EHF people in their sharp broadsides. As soon as these ugly attacks appeared, they were immediately seized upon and spread by the anti-psychic groups in mainland China, Taiwan, and Hong Kong. Anti-psychic newspapers and magazines were quick to quote them.

The reader would do well to recall the events described in chapter 4. After the anti-psychic side lost the argument, their best tactic was to seek international support to bolster their positions. Thus, at the invitation of *Science and Technology Daily*, a group of six members of the Committee for the Scientific Investigation of Claims of the Paranormal (CSICOP) visited Beijing, Xi'an, and Shanghai, and joined the ranks of the anti-psychics. But this move also provoked a backlash based on Chinese national pride. The only thing it accomplished was to add more fuel to the flames of controversy, and the anti-psychics faced criticism from more people than ever.

All along, the skeptical side in the psychic debate in China lost on the grounds that "facts beat rhetoric." They were unable to deal with the factual information. The principle proclaimed by Chinese strongman Deng Xiaoping—"The only standard in seeking the truth is practical experience"—could well be applied to the debate on the existence of psychic phenomena. The critic Yu Guangyuan's side emphasized traditional scientific beliefs (such as that the eyes are for seeing things, ears are for hearing, and so on), but stubbornly refused to look at scientific experiments which yielded data supporting psychic claims. The other side seized on these weak points relentlessly, and that led to their crushing defeat. Later, all they could do was make guerrilla attacks here and there, waiting for chances to strike back. For example, one time Zhang Baosheng's powers failed in a demonstration in Maicheng City, and the opponents made much of this, writing news reports and attacks, and giving lectures and broadcasts, anything they could do to stir up trouble. The headline on one of their articles was "Zhang Baosheng Leaves Maicheng in Defeat."

The facts of the case were these: He Zuoma, another major voice for the anti-psychic side, brought four professional magicians to observe one of Zhang Baosheng's experiments. His purpose was to show that Zhang Baosheng's EHF was fake and was no more than conjuring tricks. If he succeeded in proving fraud in this case, it would mean that this was not a scientific experiment, because science is supposed to be objective. Of course the four paid magicians came prepared for the demonstration, and insisted on many conditions and restrictions. With Zhang Baosheng's temper, he was offended by it and his bad mood affected his EHF performance level. As a result, he failed in three tests, specifically: (1) they wrote down a line from a classical poem, *"A red apricot bloom comes over the wall"* (the poem refers to a married woman having an illicit affair with her boyfriend), and placed it in an envelope, but Zhang Baosheng was unable to read it; (2) Zhang attempted to move a piece of candy into a sealed envelope, but failed; and (3) he failed in a test of removing medicine pills from a tightly sealed bottle.

After the event, their critical articles expressed the following main points. Zhang Baosheng is so presumptuous as to claim these inexplicable powers to move things with his mind, carry things through walls, see through things . . . all against the basic principles of modern physics. Not only that, he is slick enough to persuade these major scientific, political, and military institutions—which are the most scientifically oriented and don't easily lend their support to such activities, such as the Institute for Space Biology, National Security Agency, the National Science Council, and the Defense Technology Commission—to join together to sponsor EHF experimentation and observation of him . . . but in a fairly simple EHF test under strict monitoring by a few well-known scientists, he failed and was a disgrace to his country (they were referring to his being discredited to an audience with foreign observers).

The article further disclosed that a little before this, "A group of international experts (CSICOP) has made a special trip to China to investigate the claims, and all the tricks were exposed." They also noted that CSICOP had offered 10,000 U.S. dollars to anyone who proved the existence of EHF, and over a period of twenty-three years had also tested over 800 people around the world claiming to be psychics, but not one of them passed their tests and won the money. "As we see, the myths of the pseudoscience of chi gong have provoked the anger of the scientific world!" concluded the article.

The same article also charged that the effects of Yan Xin's "lecture with emitted chi" at China's old battleground, Changsha, were no more than a psychological effect and anyone could reproduce it. (This was referring to the phenomenon of members of the audience, infused with Yan Xin's chi, experiencing spontaneous body movements like swaying and shaking.)

Now, let us analyze this article's attacks, which relied on the international visitors, to judge whether they are reasonable or distorted.

First: "These Chinese claim super-psychic abilities, but their only ability is to disappear when asked to prove themselves."

The facts are: (a) Since those requested to give demonstrations knew that the Americans were well-known advocates of the anti-psychic position, they were not happy to be viewed in this hostile light. In addition, out of a sense of national pride, they were reluctant to do special performances just for the foreign group. That is why all they could do was "disappear" (or more accurately, refuse to do demonstrations for them). (b) In any country, in any field or circumstance, there are always frauds. Neither the U.S. nor China is an exception to this. When such crooks heard the foreign observers were coming to investigate them, of course they would be the first ones to disappear. In other words, those with the abilities were not willing to put themselves on display for the foreign visitors, but those without any abilities were even less willing. From another point of view, it was in the interests of the

Chinese government that the U.S. skeptics returned to their country and announced that the Chinese EHF was fake. If the U.S. security and defense agencies could be led to believe there was no need to worry about the threat of psychic war from China, they would not make preparations for it.

According to another report that has recently come into my hands, the Chinese skeptic He Zuoma discussed EHF in a lecture at China's University of Science and Technology. He said that in the recent visit by six U.S. researchers to China to investigate EHF, "to keep secrets from the Americans in certain aspects, some Chinese EHF people were not allowed to participate. . . ." The report, published in volume 158 of the news journal *Xiandai Ren* (*Modern Man*), and reprinted in *Xinwen Chuban* (*News Publication*) in the April 29, 1989, issue, is evidence enough that "security reasons" played a part in the unwillingness of some EHF supporters to let their own people with EHF cooperate with the Americans. Thus, CSICOP's people could only find some second- or third-rate people or frauds to test.

According to my own research on the case, the truly powerful psychics who refused to give demonstrations for the American skeptics had been warned ahead of time that the Americans were unfriendly. They were told that they would disrupt the demonstration in all kinds of ways, such as unfriendly remarks, nasty faces, rough movements, and many requirements and restrictions . . . which would affect the mood of the demonstrators. If the demonstrator is not in a calm and cheerful state of mind, the EHF powers will not come as easily. This is well known among psychic researchers.

Taiwan's *Lao Tian Monthly* reported on this case, "The hosts took the Americans (the CSICOP group) too seriously, and they felt the behavior was humiliating and insulting." But one of the Americans, James Randi, was of the opinion that the purpose in pursuing the inquiry so persistently was no more than to find a "simple method" of testing a child with alleged psychic powers. There has been an incident in China in which a psychic giving a demonstration of removing pills from a bottle was not in a calm mood, and one of the medicine pills went into the stomach of one of the spectators. Too much disturbance affects the mood and the performance.

Second: CSICOP has offered 10,000 U.S. dollars to anyone who proves the existence of EHF.

I would argue that nobody will ever receive this money. The reason is simple. If the testers come in with a hostile attitude, using all kinds of ways to disturb the subjects of the experiments, their EHF will never appear. Besides, the Chinese have a very strong sense of self-respect, and they are disgusted by "dollar diplomacy." The concept that "money sets all the world in motion" has long been viewed in China as a low thing like throwing a dog a bone, and will never be acceptable for them. The greatest weakness of the wealthy is the attempt to use money to lord over others. It would seem that the CSICOP team was not familiar with this aspect of Chinese thinking. The ancient Chinese wisdom says, "The rich should not be tempted by sex, the poor should not be tempted by money, and nobody should give in to bullying."

An example of this occurred in international affairs recently. In 1995, Taiwan's diplomats wanted a seat in the U.N. in exchange for one billion U.S. dollars. A billion dollars is a huge sum, and it was a time when the U.N. really needed it because it was facing financial difficulties. However, the U.N. didn't act on the offer, because it does not make its decisions that way, and it offended some people's sense of decency. Recently, pundits in the news media have been criticizing Taiwan's approach that "every man has his price" and using their prosperity as a means to fund all kinds of activities around the world in an effort to buy influence.

Third: Zhang Baosheng was accused of not only "going against the basic principles of modern physics," but also being "slick enough to persuade these major scientific, political, and military institutions—which are the most scientifically oriented and don't easily lend their support to such activities, such as the Institute for Space Biology, National Security Agency, the National Science Council, and the Defense Technology Commission—to sponsor EHF experimentation and observation of him. . . ."

This argument is particularly weak and full of holes. As we know, Zhang Baosheng was born in a village and grew up in poverty, with only a third-grade education. What kind of slickness could he have to "persuade" these four major modern institutions? The Institute for Space Biology is like a department of America's NASA, the National Security Agency is China's equivalent of the CIA, the National Science Council is headed by Dr. Qian Xuesen, China's top scientist, and the Defense Technology Commission is tasked with cutting-edge technological projects such as testing nuclear weapons and missiles. How much slickness would it take for Zhang Baosheng to persuade them? On the contrary, if these four institutions "join together to sponsor EHF experimentation and observation of him," this could be taken as evidence that his EHF is real. For example, if SRI, in Menlo Park, California, asks a person to take part in an experiment in remote viewing, we may safely assume that the scientists have some reason for selecting this person, namely that he has clairvoyant powers. Thus, I feel this line of argumentation is silly. After all, if NASA, the CIA, and the Defense Advanced Research Program joined with SRI on a psychic project, it would be a strong indication that they felt the phenomenon was real. That's the level of what happened in China.

Taiwan's *Lao Tian Monthly* said that Mr. Randi, "an expert at exposing the truth," took part in this scientific fact-finding mission with five other members, spending two weeks on a trip to far-off China "in an effort to explain several alleged psychic incidents." Isn't a mere two weeks a rather short time to spend investigating the facts about EHF in a large country? In such a short time, how many facts can one expect to learn from a whirlwind tour, or as the Chinese put it, "galloping through the flower garden on horseback"?

Fourth: The article charged that the effects in Yan Xin's "lecture with emitted chi" in Changsha were no more than a psychological effect and anyone could reproduce it.

On this issue, there are two points I need to explain. *(a)* As described in chapter 5, on several occasions when Yan Xin or other chi gong masters gave lectures with emitted chi, without their knowledge, scientists from the Chinese High Energy Physics Institute set up measuring devices, and these detected changes in the energy field. Why do the CSICOP skeptics avoid discussing this fact? *(b)* When he was in America from 1991 to 1993, Yan Xin did lectures with emitted chi many times, including some at famous universities. Why didn't the American scientists (including CSICOP members), with all their knowledge, make a scientific investigation as Yan Xin was demonstrating his alleged psychological tactics? Without going into other cases, I have attended two of Yan Xin's lectures with emitted chi at Stanford. The interpreter at the lectures was a doctor of Western medicine, and in the audience were many Californian scientists and Stanford professors, including the ones who invited Yan Xin on his visit to the U.S.A., Dr. Ken M. Sancier, retired from the research institu-

Fig. 12–1
Dr. Effie Chow (left) and Dr. Kenneth M. Sancier (right), who invited China's super psychic Yan Xin on a visit to the U.S.A.

tion SRI, who holds a Ph.D. in chemistry, and his colleague, Dr. Effie Chow. Have all of these first-rate scientists been fooled by Yan Xin?

Now, let us take a look back in time at an earlier group of U.S. scientists that went to China to investigate EHF, and what they found.

In October 1981, the State Science Commission organized a special group of seventeen people, among them American and Canadian scientists, to visit Beijing, Shanghai, and Xi'an, China, to investigate EHF. The leader was a longtime member of the Parapsychological Association, Dr. Stanley Krippner, dean of the faculty, Saybrook Institute, San Francisco. Other members included Professor Marcello Truzzi of the University of Michigan, and Dr. H. E. Puthoff, a physicist from SRI International, among others. After they arrived in China, they were welcomed by scientific institutes such as the Institute of

Paul Dong and Thomas Raffill

High Energy Physics (Beijing), Beijing Medical College, *Ziran (Nature Magazine)* (Shanghai), Beijing University, and the Institute of Traditional Chinese Medicine of Beijing. They toured China for two weeks, ran tests of twelve children, and held discussions about the ongoing development of EHF in China with the following groups and organizations.

- Beijing University physicists and biologists
- Institute of High Energy Physics
- Institute of Biophysics
- Institute of Automation
- Beijing Astronomical Observatory
- Institute of Semiconductors
- Physics Department of Beijing Teachers' College
- Institute of Traditional Chinese Medicine of Beijing

They acknowledged that China has expended great efforts in the area of EHF research, as did the children who participated in the demonstrations. However, they were not able to confirm that these children had EHF. Dr. Krippner describes all this in the afterword of my book, *The Four Major Mysteries of Mainland China*. Dr. Puthoff has also made a detailed description of this in his "Report on Investigations Into 'Exceptional Human Functions' in the People's Republic of China" written for the Institute of Noetic Sciences (Spring 1983). Professor Truzzi, in turn, published a report in *Omni* and *Zetetic Scholar*, where he is editor.

As a result of this U.S.–China scientific exchange, they have all become good friends. At the Conference Celebrating the 100th Anniversary of the British Society for Psychical Research at Trinity College, Cambridge, England, August 16–20, 1982, two Chinese conferees from the Institute of Aerospace Medico-Engineering, Beijing—Professor Chen Xin and Professor Mei Lei—were in attendance. Dr. Puthoff's report also tells of these results.

It is particularly worth mentioning Dr. Puthoff, a very good friend. For many years now, I have been trying to explain the phenomenon of "chi" in Chinese chi gong in terms of the Western scientific outlook. Dr. Puthoff, with his broad knowledge, has often asked me to explain about chi. He believes that chi could be "zero-point energy." He has studied zero-point energy for many years with some good results.

Having come to this point, we still have not answered the question: Did the Chinese children really have EHF or didn't they?

Before attempting to reach a conclusion, let us consider something else. Have you ever had an experience in which you noticed the effects of your mood on the outcome? Earlier, I have described the manner of the CSICOP delegation's hostile and demanding attitude, which resulted in the EHF children failing in their demonstrations. But the situation was different for this friendly group of visitors.

I recall when I was nine years old, I left my village in China to go to town to see the doctor. I was admitted into a hospital run by Christian missionaries from England. Then I had an operation on my back. For a few days after the surgery, I had to take painkillers every morning. One morning, before I had taken my medicine, two missionaries visited me in the hospital room. The two were English ladies. After coming in, they greeted me, held my hand, and chatted with me. They knew I couldn't understand English, but they wanted to bring goodwill to the patients, to comfort them. In the ten to fifteen minutes they were in the hospital room, my pain went away. My mother later told me about this.

Of course, they did not have EHF. What stopped my pain was not psychic powers, but the distraction of my attention.

I was born in the countryside, and this was the first time I saw the big city, Guangzhou. It was also the first time I saw Caucasians. They were physically larger than Chinese, had blond hair, blue eyes, and very big noses (compared with Chinese people). Their faces were pale with pinkish tinges. At the time, I thought to myself, "So there are such beautiful people in the world." The two missionaries spoke English, which sounded like bird chirping to me. . . . All these things attracted me, a feeling of surprise rose up in my heart, and so I recovered from my pain without any medication.

The above description is one of the key factors in the failure of the Chinese children before the audience of Westerners. Of course, there were other causes besides that. For example, one thing the Chinese fear most is to "lose face to the foreigners." They feel that it is more disgraceful to fail in front of foreigners. The more you fear failure, the more likely you are to fail. Clearly, the enlightened U.S. and Canadian scientists were aware of this effect, but didn't want to say anything about it. This is because there are times when the more you try to explain something, the more you mix things up and make matters worse. It might have made people suspect that they were trying to cover up for the children's failure. Scientific experiments are generally black-and-white, giving either positive or negative results, and there can be no excuses for failure.

As to the question whether China's psychic children are real or fake, this is not the suitable place to argue it. The best we can do is to present facts and let these facts speak for themselves. In the summer of 1985, five years after the U.S.–Canadian fact-finding mission went to China, and three years after the CSICOP team's trip, Hong Kong and Japan organized a trip by a group of journalists to go to mainland China to investigate EHF, also focusing on the children. Their first stop was Shanghai, where they immediately tested seven EHF children. This group of children was assembled by the editor for *Nature Magazine*, Miss Zhu Yiyi. They were Li Xia (female, fifteen), Sun Huafeng (male, twenty), Wang Xiaohong (female, fourteen), Zhao Xun (male, fifteen), Song Hongmei (female, fifteen), Zhang Jing (female, fifteen), and Xu Huizhen (female, sixteen).

They first tested reading with the ear and the armpit. The subjects of this test were Li Xia and Zhao Xun. They had 100 percent success rates. The next test was breaking objects by mind power, on subjects Zhang Jing, Xu Huizhen, and Wang Xiaohong. The three of them held test tubes containing iron wires. After fourteen minutes, all the iron wires were bent. The third test, on subject Sun Huafeng, was "removing pills from bottles." In five minutes, at first one pill fell out, and, after a pause, many more came after it.

The above tests seemed to go so smoothly that the Japanese journalists were skeptical. The next day, at their suggestion, stricter procedures were followed, including pretest body searches and strict monitoring of all their movements. After several tests, the Japanese journalists were fully convinced and were in awe.

In the period from 1981 to 1988, at least twenty groups from Hong Kong, Taiwan, and Japan visited mainland China to investigate EHF. Believe it or not, not one of them said there was a "failure." It is particularly noteworthy that the reporters from Hong Kong and Taiwan were not very favorable to China and couldn't be expected to say nice things about China.

The virtues of modesty, sincerity, honesty, kindness, and consideration, treasured by the Chinese people for thousands of years, were all broken by a bunch of unscrupulous people. To protect their own images, they attacked the exercise sys-

Paul Dong and Thomas Raffill

tem of chi gong—recognized as having health benefits for 3,000 years by the Buddhist, Taoist, and Confucian medical traditions—as a "pseudoscience." Teaming up with Americans, they published a book strongly attacking chi gong, which is loved by most people in China. Why?

Over the past decade, chi gong has attained great popularity in China. Many experts, scholars, and medical researchers have gone to China to learn about Chinese medicine and chi gong, and they have confirmed its value. For this reason, at least fifteen chi gong books have been published in England and America. At the same time, there is one book calling chi gong a "pseudoscience." Are the authors' faces red?

• 13 •

The Psychics of Taiwan

Taiwan is a Chinese island located in the South China Sea about 150 nautical miles from the coast of China. Its current population is 20 million, which is only about two-thirds of the population of a typical province in China. In proportion to this, the number of psychics is also fewer, but among them are some of the most striking examples of people with EHF. Taiwan also has a Society of Parapsychology Research, with around six hundred members.

Taiwan has few people with natural-born EHF abilities, but they also lack the techniques for developing them through chi gong. On the other hand, the people of Taiwan have many superstitions and beliefs of a spiritual or religious nature, particularly Buddhism and "native spirits." In the most recent couple of election campaigns for president of Taiwan, there have been Buddhist and Catholic candidates. In order to win votes, the latter often visited Buddhist temples and shrines to worship. This gives an indication of how widespread such beliefs are in Taiwan.

As we know, superstitions and spiritual beliefs can also give rise to EHF. Some people who develop EHF powers through such beliefs try to turn themselves into gods. These people sometimes claim to be incarnations of the gods, or to be inhabited by the spirits of gods, and use this as a means to get rich at the expense of the public. As we write this chapter, Taiwan is going through two scandals related to fraudulent acquisition of wealth in this manner, involving amounts equivalent to tens of millions in U.S. dollars.

Even though Taiwan is full of temples to Buddha, and the people are superstitious, at the same time, people look down on parapsychological research. It was not until 1976 that a group of scholars got together to organize a parapsychology association. They applied to the government for a permit to establish the organization, but reportedly their application was approved only with difficulty, after one year. Since then, they have been publishing the journal of their society, *Chao Xinli Xue Yanjiu* (*Parapsychology Research*).

Professor Huang Dashou, who has taught in Central University, was elected chairman of the society and editor-in-chief of their journal. Other members of the association include Professor Wang Shaolun of Taiwan Teachers' College, Professor Zang Guangen, who teaches in Japan, Professor Xu Dingming, Professor Zhao Ji, and Professor Shi Chaolin. They are underfunded and carry out their work with great difficulty in poor conditions.

After the rise of widespread interest in EHF in mainland China, Professor Huang Dashou has given very serious attention to the human body science promulgated by Dr. Qian Xuesen, and he also has frequent contacts with chi gong and EHF circles in mainland China. He has also sponsored visits to Taiwan by mainland China's researchers. It is particularly noteworthy that Professor Huang, in spite of his advanced age and frail health, has made many trips to mainland China to visit the human body science and chi gong research associations and EHF people, including Zhang Baosheng.

Shi Chaolin has been hailed as "Taiwan's Zhang Baosheng." An interesting story about him dates to August 25, 1984. Shi Chaolin was taking a vacation in Las Vegas, Nevada, with a businessman named Zhang. Right at the outset, the businessman lost large amounts of money. Half seriously, he asked Shi, "Can you win my money back with your psychic abilities?"

"I can try," replied Shi Chaolin. "Let's start with this slot machine," he added.

And so they picked at random a 25-cent slot machine. The businessman fed it quarters and operated it while Shi Chaolin used his mind power to will the money in the machine to pour out. Suddenly, all the money came out of the machine at once. The machine wouldn't stop clattering.

In the casino, the clatter of a slot machine is a common occurrence, and so it didn't attract much attention. Neighboring gamblers did no more than to say, "You're lucky."

They saw the experiment was a success, and thought it would be a good idea to try again. They chose another slot machine and worked it the same way as before. But this time the results were astounding. Perhaps this machine was filled with more than the usual amount of coins. The coins rolled out furiously, and attracted a crowd of gamblers. Among them were some casino employees. One of the casino bankers took them to the office. The manager asked them what they were doing, where they came from, and how they got all the money out of the machine. He had questions to ask. Then, Shi Chaolin gave the manager his card. His card identified him as "Member of the Parapsychology Association of the Republic of China." (Note: The institutions on Taiwan are referred to as the "Republic of China," not to be confused with the "People's Republic" on the mainland.) After reading it, the manager said, "If you want to do experiments on psychic power, go to your laboratory. You can't play tricks like this in our casino." The manager and the banker, who had a gun, had tough looks on their faces. It seemed they were in trouble, but just as they were bemoaning their fate, the flashbulbs of a group of journalists started popping. Whether by coincidence or by good luck, the group of journalists was passing through the casino just at that moment and helped them to escape from a dangerous situation.

Shi Chaolin was born with this kind of power. He remembers the time when his grandfather was playing cards, and he was watching from behind. His grandfather was losing every time, and when that happened, he would concentrate his mind and wish for his grandfather to win. Then, his grandfather really did win. It worked like this time after time, and he thought it was strange. Once, he wished for another person to win, and the other person did win. Since that time, he has known he had psychic powers. In the years that followed, he became interested in fortune telling, *feng shui* (Chinese geomancy, or the practice of arranging a place to harmonize the spirits), and the ancient Chinese traditions of numerology, and became a well-known expert in these fields.

Nor is Shi Chaosen the only Chinese to have won money in Las Vegas by using psychic ability. Another super psychic, mainland China's Chen Zhu, also went to the world-famous casinos of Las Vegas, winning eight million U.S. dollars. As reported in the Chinese-language U.S. newpaper, *Shijie Ribao* (*World Journal*) of May 13, 1997, Chen Zhu disclosed that he had won eight million dollars in the Monte Carlo. In the end, the manager made him agree he would not come more than once every four months [author's note: the report quoting four months may have been a misprint for four years, since they couldn't afford to drop eight million dollars every four months]. The report did not say what game he played to win eight million dollars, but to our knowledge, Chen Zhu is most famous for playing blackjack. In Macao (a gambling town one hour's trip by boat from Hong Kong) he once won forty games in a row. At blackjack, he could go on winning thousands of times. He uses his mind power to change the cards dealt to him at will. One time, he did an experiment in front of TV cameras, allowing six members of the audience to pick three cards from a deck. When they turned the cards over, all of them had twenty-one! If the manager of the Monte Carlo didn't believe this, his casino would lose money. Chen Zhu had come to the U.S. before. He often said, "Americans don't believe in EHF." Was the manager of the Monte Carlo one of these? Mainland Chinese publications have said that American skeptics of EHF who saw his activities believed only God could have the power to do the things he did.

World Journal also said that Chen Zhu accepted an invitation to be one of the performers in the ceremony commemorating the return of Hong Kong to Chinese rule on July 1, 1997.

Taiwan has a hypnotist, Professor Xu Dingming, also a member of the parapsychology association. When he was young, his mother suffered from sciatic neuralgia. She tried many doctors with no success. When he was fourteen, he saw an advertisement and signed up for correspondence classes with Dr. Bao Fangzhou, a nationally famous hypnotist at that time (I also took correspondence classes from him thirty years ago). In a short time, he learned hypnotic induction, and he used what he had learned on his mother. It worked, and his mother recovered without the need for any further treatment.

From then on, he made great efforts to learn hypnotism, so that today, he is the most famous hypnotist in Taiwan. He coined a new term called "*ling li* human electric therapy." *Ling li*, or "spirit power," refers to psychic power or mind power. Human electricity is something like the body's static electricity, but it is not easy to translate into English. Actually, taken as a whole, the term refers to psychic power, but it is dressed up with fancy words like human electricity. As we know, some people like to create new terms when they have succeeded in something, to show people what a high level they have attained. In fact, hypnotism, induction, the power of faith, and spirit superstitions are all different types of psychic phenomena.

Professor Xu has cured many people with his therapy based on hypnotic suggestion. Once, someone asked him if all his patients were cured. He openly admitted that it wasn't 100 percent effective, and that it depended on the sensitivity of the subject to human electricity (or chi). The effects are better for those sensitive to the energy, just as is the case with chi gong healing. The problem is that there are some fakes in the world who make exaggerated claims and say they can cure anybody. And just because it sometimes happens that therapy by a hypnotist or chi gong master is not effective, skeptics use this to attack it as fraud and pseudoscience.

Because Professor Xu's fame is so high in Taiwan, he has authored twenty-five books in over four decades, including three relating to law enforcement and security issues, *Spirituality in Police Training*, *Lectures on Spirituality for Military Police*, and *The Significance of Parapsychology in Modern National Defense*. Actually, the twenty-five works are more like long essays, because they are all slim volumes without much research information. His 1984 book *Chinese Psychic Healing* was translated by Francis T. S. Hung and James A. Decker, and Professor Cyrus Lee (Li Shaokun) of Edinboro University of Pennsylvania wrote the foreword to it.

From July to September 1983, Professor Xu hosted Professor Li in his Spirit Healing Seminar. They got along well together, and so they formed a Sino-American Psychic Research Institute.

Recently I spent an hour reading through Professor Xu's 1974 book *The Significance of Parapsychology in Modern National Defense*. The second chapter, "Japan Uses Parapsychology Heavily in National Security," presents the claim that in the Russo-Japanese War, Japan used psychics trained by the "silent sitting" meditation technique of Wang Yangming (an ancient Chinese master) to determine the numbers and movements of the Russian fleet, which they succeeded in catching and destroying. The chief of staff of the Japanese navy at the time, Akiyama Saneyuki, once told this to the founder of the Republic of China, Dr. Sun Yat-sen. Records of this can also be found in the writings left by Dr. Sun Yatsen.

During the war between Russia and Japan, which lasted from February 1904 to September 1905, the technique used by Japan was hypnosis, and some of the people tasked to this mission included the well-known Ms. Mifune Senzuko, Lieutenant Sakurai, and hypnotist Okada Yoshinori. In that period, they didn't know how to train for psychic abilities. Later they learned of the work done by the Soviets and the U.S. in this field. At present, Japan is studying the Chinese chi gong training method. Japan has sent many groups and individuals, of civilian status, to China to study all kinds of chi gong and to observe the prevailing conditions and state of development of EHF in China. They also often invite famous Chinese chi gong masters to Japan to demonstrate and lecture.

Chapter 5 of the same work, "Red China's Research in Spiritualism and Experiments in Telepathy," states that mainland China conducted an experiment in "telepathy" between the cities of Beijing and Kunming in 1971. ("Telepathy" is used here in a broad sense to refer to any spiritual communication, including the "thousand-mile eye and ear" remote perception modes as well as thought transference.) The source he cited for this information was *Telepathic Strategies in the U.S. and Russia*, published in December 1974 by Nihon Tairiku Shobo Company and written by Ichimura Toshihiko. The book was obviously about U.S. and Russian security issues, and may only have briefly mentioned China's "telepathic" experiment, but no matter whether it mentioned it in passing or gave a detailed account, not a bit of it is to be believed. Ichimura may have been sensationalizing the Chinese "telepathy" to promote sales by making his book more exciting to the public.

Another possibility is that the Japanese government was behind this, because whenever Japanese institutions want to do something, they tend to accuse others of doing it as a means to cover their real purposes. With the Chinese telepathic experiments, they may have been concealing their own psychic experiments. A good example of this type of behavior took place in 1994, when the Japanese published a document called *On the Chinese Threat*, which presented the thesis that China was gradually becoming stronger and would dominate the scene in the coming millennium, posing a threat to other countries in the East Asian and Southeast Asian regions. After it was released, people in other regional countries began decrying the "Chinese threat."

The Chinese countered this by pointing out that in the half century since Japan's defeat in World War II, the country had rebuilt itself into an economic superpower, with annual defense expenditures second only to those of the U.S. Its militaristic and nationalistic traditions led it to build massive naval, ground, and air forces, which already posed a terrifying threat to East and Southeast Asian countries. This convincing refutation shows how the Japanese used the "Chinese threat" as a pretext, camouflaging their own aggressive agenda to rebuild their country as the major regional power.

We would agree with the Chinese government's position on this. Until 1979, mainland China not only had no understanding of psychic powers, during the decade of the rule by the Gang of Four, EHF was prohibited. Such areas of the spirit and soul were labeled as metaphysical idealism and denounced as decadent and pseudoscientific. Even to this day (1997), mainland China has many traditional scientists who oppose EHF and denounce its research as "pseudoscience."

In a way the Japanese could not have anticipated, since the authorities of mainland China became aware of EHF in 1979, they have pursued its research vigorously and surpassed Japan itself, which had been ahead in psychic research for the previous three decades. Although the story of the Chinese test of telepathy from Beijing to Kunming in 1971 may have been a pure fabrication, in an interesting coincidence, on the eve of the new year in 1986, twenty scientists from Qinghua University and other Chinese institutions really did do such a test from Beijing to Kunming, a distance of 2,000 kilometers. The Japanese would never have imagined this thirty years before.

Another story from Taiwan could be even more fascinating than these stories from Xu Dingming. In 1986, Taiwan author Zhang Xiguo wrote *Qi Wang* (*Chess King*), a story about a boy who could see the future. He could tell what would happen on the next day, and also could tell what was happening to other people. Sometimes he would predict the fluctuations in stock-market prices. This story was later made into a film that aroused a great deal of interest. Just as everyone was discussing it, a sixteen-year-old girl in Taizhong, Taiwan, was discovered to have similar abilities. She wished to remain anonymous, and so we refer to her as Miss Ann from here on.

Miss Ann was discovered by a fortune teller, Mr. Zhang. He was quite well known, because he often published articles in the newspapers on Chinese astrology, reading people's fates by calculations from their date of birth.

One afternoon, responding to a newspaper advertisement with Mr. Zhang's address, Miss Ann visited him. Mr. Zhang thought she had come for a reading and asked her to sit down. Then Miss Ann said, "Mr. Zhang, I have not come for you to tell my fortune. I have come to tell your fortune." The tone was serious, but the words were coming from a young lady. Mr. Zhang was unsure of what to say to this.

"Here is how it is," she said. "I always read your articles. After I read yesterday's article, I dreamed of something that happened in your past." At this point, her voice went soft, with a tone that sounded sympathetic.

"You did business, but failed in it, and failed miserably. In order to make your living, you were forced to turn to fortune telling."

The fortune teller listened to these words coming from a stranger, and felt that she was no ordinary girl. She must be a wonder child!

On closer questioning, Miss Ann told him the whole story. She often dreamed about things that happened to people, and later they all turned out to be true. For example, before May 16, 1985, when Hong Kong film starlet Weng Meiling committed suicide by taking an overdose of drugs, she had dreamed of it. She said, brokenheartedly, "Mr. Zhang, I am so unhappy. I am a big fan of hers. I should have told her long ago and stopped her. She could have avoided this awful end."

Miss Ann also dreamed of her grandfather's death, and typhoons and floods in Taiwan. All of them came true. At first, people didn't believe her, and by the time they did, it was too late.

In recent years, Miss Ann has sometimes been able to see into the future when she is thinking deeply. The ability has become stronger and stronger, but it has disturbed her peace. Greedy friends and relatives always asked her to pick lucky numbers for them for the "All Happy" game (a kind of sweepstakes, lottery or lotto, in Taiwan). Too many people she met asked her for help, and she got no rest. She was becoming more tired and gaining more weight every day.

After a year of this, she visited Mr. Zhang again and complained to him, saying she regretted that she had not listened to his warning not to tell others about her EHF, for fear that her friends or bad people would try to use her. Because she was so young and inexperienced, she was unable to keep her secret.

This teenage Miss Taiwan hit the jackpot four times in the "All Happy" game!

Index

INDEX

INDEX

INDEX

INDEX

INDEX

INDEX

INDEX

INDEX

PAUL DONG is an internationally known writer and editor in the fields of unexplained and paranormal phenomena. He was born in Canton, China, in 1928. He is now an American citizen and resides in Oakland, California, with his wife and children where he is actively engaged in journalism and scientific research. Since 1976 he has been a chi gong instructor at the San Francisco YMCA and the San Francisco College of Acupuncture. He is also an avid researcher into psychic and paranormal phenomena.

Mr. Dong has close ties with Chinese scientific circles and is editor-in-chief of the *Journal of UFO Research*, a bimonthly magazine published in mainland China with a circulation of more than 300,000. As a journalist, he has published articles in Hong Kong, Japan, Germany, England, and the U.S. His article "Mainland Mystery" was published in the May 1981 issue of *Omni*.

In addition to his articles, he is author of the *The Four Major Mysteries of Mainland China* (Prentice-Hall, 1984), coauthor of *Chi Gong—The Ancient Chinese Way to Health* (Marlowe and Company, 1990), and *Empty Force* (Element Books, England, 1996).

THOMAS RAFFILL, a native of Oakland, California, is a translator and consultant who has worked in international matters both for government and private business. Since 1987 he has been a student of Master Paul Dong in the meditation practice of chi gong. A graduate of the University of California at

Berkeley, he is fluent in the Chinese, Japanese, and Russian languages, and has traveled extensively in the Eastern world, including visits to China, Japan, and Russia for research purposes.

Mr. Raffill practices chi gong every day and uses it for self-healing and personal development. He has witnessed many demonstrations of mysterious energies and is convinced of their potential as healing powers.